Preface

This book is your companion on a journey through the intricate and dynamic world of MySQL Text Book, an open-source relational database management system that has captivated the hearts of developers, database administrators, and businesses worldwide.

In a data-driven era where information is the lifeblood of organizations, mastering a robust and versatile database system like MySQL is of paramount importance. This book is tailored to meet the diverse needs of readers, whether you're taking your first steps into the realm of databases or you're an experienced database professional looking to deepen your MySQL expertise.

This book covers a wide range of topics, starting with the foundational concepts of databases and gradually progressing to advanced techniques and emerging trends. Here's a glimpse of what you can expect:

Clarity and Depth: We break down complex concepts into manageable pieces, ensuring you can grasp the intricacies of MySQL while building a strong foundation of understanding.

Practical Experience: Real-world examples and hands-on exercises help you apply MySQL concepts in practical scenarios, from designing efficient databases to optimizing performance.

Comprehensive Coverage: Whether you're interested in SQL queries, database design, stored procedures, or advanced topics like replication and cloud integration, this book covers it all.

Best Practices: Throughout the book, we emphasize best practices for MySQL development, administration, and security.

A Learning Journey: We've structured the content to take you from MySQL basics to advanced techniques, allowing you to grow your skills at your own pace.

As you navigate through these pages, you'll find the collective wisdom of experienced database professionals, developers, and MySQL enthusiasts who have contributed to this comprehensive resource.

We'd like to express our gratitude to the MySQL community, whose passion and dedication have played an instrumental role in shaping this book. We'd also like to thank our families, friends, and colleagues for their unwavering support throughout this endeavour.

We believe that this book will be a valuable resource on your journey to becoming a MySQL master. Whether you're a student, a professional, or an enthusiast, we hope this book equips you with the knowledge and skills you need to harness the full potential of MySQL.

Thank you for choosing this book as your guide to the fascinating world of MySQL. Let's embark on this MySQL adventure together!

Table of Contents

Chapter 1: Introduction to MySQL

1.1 History and Background

MySQL is an open-source relational database management system (RDBMS) that has played a significant role in the world of database technology. Its history and background are characterized by innovation, open-source collaboration, and widespread adoption. Here's a brief overview:

Inception (Mid-1990s): MySQL was initially developed by a Swedish company called MySQL AB, founded by Michael Widenius, David Axmark, and Allan Larsson in the mid-1990s. It was created as a result of the founders' desire to create a database system that was both efficient and open-source.

Naming Inspiration: The name "MySQL" is a combination of "My," the daughter of co-founder Michael Widenius, and "SQL," which stands for Structured Query Language. It reflects the system's origins as a small-scale project.

Open-Source Commitment: MySQL was one of the early pioneers of open-source database systems. From the beginning, it was distributed under an open-source license, which contributed to its rapid adoption by developers and organizations.

Growth and Popularity (Late 1990s - Early 2000s): MySQL gained popularity in the late 1990s and early 2000s due to its ease of use, speed, and reliability. It became a popular choice for web applications, powering websites and applications across various industries.

Acquisition by Sun Microsystems (2008): In 2008, Sun Microsystems acquired MySQL AB for approximately $1 billion. This acquisition aimed to strengthen Sun's position in the open-source software market and broaden its software portfolio.

Oracle Corporation's Ownership (2010): Shortly after the Sun Microsystems acquisition, Oracle Corporation acquired Sun, including MySQL. This move raised concerns in the open-source community about the future of MySQL, but Oracle made commitments to continue developing and supporting it.

MySQL Forks and Diversification: In response to concerns about MySQL's future under Oracle, several forks and alternative MySQL-based database systems emerged. Notable forks include MariaDB and Percona Server. These projects aimed to maintain a free and open-source version of MySQL.

MySQL as a Part of Oracle Corporation: Despite concerns, MySQL has continued to be actively developed and maintained by Oracle Corporation. It has seen significant improvements, including the introduction of features for scalability, high availability, and security.

Community and Enterprise Editions: MySQL offers both a Community Edition, which is open-source and free to use, and an Enterprise Edition with additional features and support options for commercial users.

Widespread Adoption: MySQL is widely adopted and used by organizations of all sizes, from startups to large enterprises. It is favoured for web applications, content management systems (CMS), e-commerce platforms, and data-driven applications.

Today, MySQL remains one of the most popular and widely used relational database management systems globally, serving as the foundation for numerous web-based applications and services. Its history reflects the enduring appeal of open-source software and the importance of relational databases in modern computing.

1.2 MySQL Editions and Versions

MySQL, an open-source relational database management system (RDBMS), is available in various editions and versions to cater to the diverse needs of users, from individual developers to large enterprises. Here's an overview of the editions and versions of MySQL:

Editions:

MySQL Community Edition:

The MySQL Community Edition is the free and open-source version of MySQL.

It is suitable for developers, small-scale projects, and organizations that prefer open-source solutions.

It includes essential features for database management, data storage, and query processing.

Community support is available through forums, documentation, and open-source communities.

MySQL Enterprise Edition:

The MySQL Enterprise Edition is a commercial offering from Oracle Corporation.

It is designed for enterprises and mission-critical applications that require advanced features, support, and additional tools.

Key features include advanced security, high availability, scalability, backup, and monitoring tools.

It offers premium support, including 24/7 support from MySQL experts.

Versions:

MySQL versions are identified by a combination of a major version number and a minor version number (e.g., MySQL 8.0). Each version may introduce new features, improvements, and bug fixes. Here are some notable MySQL versions:

MySQL 5.5:

Introduced in 2010.

Notable features included performance improvements, semi-synchronous replication, and InnoDB enhancements.

MySQL 5.6:

Released in 2013.

Introduced features like NoSQL support with the InnoDB storage engine, improved performance, and enhanced security.

MySQL 5.7:

Released in 2015.

Major improvements in security with features like native password hashing and role-based access control.

Enhanced JSON support and performance enhancements.

MySQL 8.0:

Released in 2018.

Major enhancements, including support for common table expressions (CTEs), window functions, and improved performance.

Increased security features, including the MySQL Authentication Plugin and password policy improvements.

MySQL 8.0.23 and Beyond:

Subsequent updates and maintenance releases have continued to improve performance, security, and functionality.

MySQL continues to evolve with ongoing development and community contributions.

Users can choose the MySQL edition and version that best suits their requirements based on factors such as scalability, security, support, and licensing. It's essential to stay informed about the latest MySQL releases to take advantage of new features and improvements while ensuring compatibility with existing applications and systems.

1.3 MySQL Architecture Overview

MySQL, like most relational database management systems (RDBMS), follows a client-server architecture. It consists of various components that work together to store, manage, and retrieve data efficiently. Here's an overview of the key components and their roles in MySQL's architecture:

Client: The client is an application or program that interacts with the MySQL database server. Clients can be anything from a command-line interface (CLI) tool to a web application or a desktop application. They send SQL queries and commands to the server for data manipulation and retrieval.

Server: The MySQL server is the core of the database system. It's responsible for managing data, processing queries, and handling connections from clients. The server's components include:

SQL Interface: This component receives SQL queries from clients and processes them. It includes a SQL parser and query optimizer, which analyse and optimize queries for efficient execution.

Storage Engine: MySQL supports multiple storage engines, such as InnoDB, MyISAM, and more. The storage engine is responsible for managing how data is stored on disk, including data indexing, transactions, and locking mechanisms. InnoDB is the default storage engine in recent MySQL versions due to its reliability and support for transactions.

Query Cache: MySQL can cache query results to improve query performance. When a client sends a query, the server checks if the result is already in the cache and, if so, returns it without re-executing the query.

Connection Handler: This component manages client connections to the server. It handles tasks like authentication, access control, and connection pooling.

Buffer Pool: MySQL uses a buffer pool to cache frequently used data pages in memory. This cache helps reduce disk I/O, improving query performance.

Log Files: MySQL maintains various log files, including the binary log, error log, and slow query log. These logs record important information for debugging, replication, and auditing purposes.

Data Directory: This is the directory on the server's file system where MySQL stores its data files. Each database and table has a corresponding file or set of files in this directory.

System Catalog (Information Schema): MySQL maintains a system catalog called the information schema, which stores metadata about databases, tables, columns, and other database objects. It provides a structured way to query and retrieve information about the database schema.

SQL Layer: The SQL layer is responsible for parsing SQL statements, optimizing query execution plans, and handling query execution. It interacts with the storage engines to retrieve or modify data.

Connection Pool: Many MySQL servers use a connection pool to manage client connections efficiently. The connection pool maintains a set of pre-established connections that can be reused, reducing the overhead of establishing and tearing down connections for each client request.

Understanding the MySQL architecture is essential for database administrators, developers, and system administrators to optimize performance, troubleshoot issues, and design scalable and reliable database systems. The choice of storage engine, server configuration, and query optimization strategies all play a crucial role in MySQL's overall performance and behavior.

1.4 Licensing and Installation

The MySQL website (http://www.mysql.com/) provides the latest information about MySQL software.

MySQL is available under various licensing options, with the most common being the open-source General Public License (GPL). The licensing model and installation process may vary depending on whether you're using the MySQL Community Edition or the MySQL Enterprise Edition. Here's an overview of MySQL's licensing and installation:

Licensing:

MySQL Community Edition:

The MySQL Community Edition is licensed under the open-source GNU General Public License (GPL). This means you can use, modify, and distribute it freely without cost.

You can download, install, and use the MySQL Community Edition for a wide range of applications, including personal projects, small businesses, and non-commercial use.

The GPL license requires that any modifications you make to the MySQL source code must also be made available under the GPL when distributed.

MySQL Enterprise Edition:

The MySQL Enterprise Edition is a commercial offering from Oracle Corporation.

It includes additional features, support, and tools for enterprises and mission-critical applications.
Licensing for the MySQL Enterprise Edition typically involves purchasing a subscription or licenses based on your organization's needs.
Subscriptions often include access to technical support, certified software, and monitoring and management tools.

Installation:

The installation process for MySQL can vary slightly depending on your operating system, but here are general steps for installing MySQL:

Download MySQL:

Visit the official MySQL website (https://dev.mysql.com/downloads/) to download the MySQL Community Edition or MySQL Enterprise Edition based on your requirements.
Select the appropriate version for your operating system (e.g., Windows, Linux, macOS).

Installation on Windows:

For Windows users, MySQL provides an installer that simplifies the installation process. Run the installer and follow the on-screen instructions.
During installation, you can configure various options, such as setting the root password, choosing a storage engine, and selecting components to install.

Installation on Linux:

On Linux, you can often use package managers like APT (Debian/Ubuntu) or YUM (Red Hat/CentOS) to install MySQL. For example:

"sudo apt-get install mysql-server"

After installation, you may need to start the MySQL service and enable it to start automatically on system boot.

Configuration:

Once MySQL is installed, you may need to configure it based on your specific requirements. Configuration files are typically located in the MySQL data directory.
Important configuration options include setting up security, defining storage engines, and configuring system variables.

Testing and Verification:

After installation and configuration, it's essential to test the MySQL server to ensure it's running correctly.
You can use the MySQL command-line client or graphical tools like MySQL Workbench to connect to the server and execute SQL queries.

Securing MySQL:

For security reasons, it's crucial to secure your MySQL installation. This includes setting strong passwords, limiting user access, and applying security best practices.
MySQL installation can vary in complexity based on your specific needs and the chosen edition (Community or Enterprise). It's recommended to refer to the official MySQL documentation for detailed installation instructions and specific considerations for your operating system and edition.

1.5 How MySQL Can Help You

MySQL is a powerful open-source relational database management system (RDBMS) that can provide several benefits to individuals, businesses, and organizations. Here are detailed ways in which MySQL can help you:

Data Management:

MySQL allows you to efficiently store, manage, and retrieve your data. You can create multiple databases and tables to organize your information systematically.

Cost-Effective:

MySQL is open-source and free to use, making it a cost-effective choice for businesses, especially startups and small organizations.

High Performance:

MySQL is known for its excellent performance. It can handle large amounts of data and concurrent users without significant performance degradation.

Scalability:

MySQL is highly scalable. You can start with a small database and scale it up as your data requirements grow. This is crucial for businesses that anticipate expansion.

Security:

MySQL provides robust security features, including user authentication, authorization, and encryption. It helps protect your data from unauthorized access and breaches.

Reliability:

MySQL is known for its reliability and stability. It has been widely used for many years and has a proven track record in various industries.

ACID Compliance:

MySQL follows the ACID (Atomicity, Consistency, Isolation, Durability) properties, ensuring that your data remains consistent and reliable, even in the event of system failures.

Flexibility:

MySQL supports various data types, including numeric, string, date, and time. You can work with structured data, unstructured data, and even binary data.

Support for Transactions:

MySQL supports transactions, which are crucial for applications that require multiple related database operations to be executed as a single unit. This ensures data integrity.

Indexing:

MySQL offers efficient indexing mechanisms, such as B-tree and hash indexes, to speed up data retrieval. This is vital for databases with large datasets.

Replication and High Availability:

MySQL supports replication, allowing you to create copies of your database for load balancing or disaster recovery. High availability solutions are also available.

Backup and Recovery:

MySQL provides tools for data backup and recovery, ensuring that you can restore your database to a previous state in case of data loss or corruption.

Community and Support:

MySQL has a large and active community of users and developers. You can find extensive documentation, tutorials, and support from the community.

Integration:

MySQL integrates well with various programming languages, making it suitable for web applications, content management systems, e-commerce platforms, and more.

Customization:

MySQL allows you to customize your database system with plugins and extensions, tailoring it to your specific needs.

Open Standards:

MySQL complies with SQL standards, making it compatible with other RDBMS systems and ensuring portability of your database.

Data Warehousing:

MySQL can be used in data warehousing solutions to store and analyze large volumes of data, making it valuable for business intelligence and analytics.

Web Development:

MySQL is often used with web development technologies like PHP, Python, and JavaScript to power dynamic web applications.

In summary, MySQL is a versatile and reliable database management system that can help you effectively store, manage, and secure your data, whether for personal use, small businesses, or large enterprises. Its open-source nature, coupled with a robust feature set, makes it a popular choice for a wide range of applications.

1.6 Basic Database Terminology

Understanding basic database terminology in MySQL is essential for effectively working with databases. Here are detailed explanations of key terms:

Database:

A database is a structured collection of data organized into tables, rows, and columns. In MySQL, a database contains data and can include multiple tables.

Table:

A table is a fundamental database object in MySQL. It represents a structured set of data organized into rows and columns. Each table has a name and a defined schema that specifies the data types for each column.

Row (Record):

A row, also known as a record, is a horizontal entry in a table. It contains data values for each column, corresponding to a single entity or record.

Column (Field):

A column, also known as a field, is a vertical element within a table that represents a specific data attribute. Each column has a data type that defines the kind of data it can hold.

Primary Key:

A primary key is a unique identifier for each row in a table. It enforces data integrity by ensuring that each record can be uniquely identified. Primary keys are often used for referencing records in other tables.

Foreign Key:

A foreign key is a field in one table that links to the primary key in another table. It establishes relationships between tables, enforcing referential integrity and enabling the creation of complex queries.

Index:

An index is a database structure that enhances data retrieval performance by creating a sorted list of values from one or more columns. Indexes speed up the process of searching and filtering data.

Query:

A query is a request for data manipulation or retrieval from a database. MySQL supports SQL (Structured Query Language) for creating and executing queries.

SQL (Structured Query Language):

SQL is a domain-specific language used for managing and querying relational databases. It includes commands for creating, modifying, and querying database structures and data.

Normalization:

Normalization is the process of organizing data in a database to minimize data redundancy and improve data integrity. It involves breaking down tables into smaller, related tables and defining relationships.

Denormalization:

Denormalization is the opposite of normalization. It involves intentionally introducing redundancy into a database to optimize query performance. It's often used in data warehousing.

Transaction:

A transaction is a sequence of one or more SQL statements that are executed as a single unit of work. Transactions ensure the database remains in a consistent state, following the ACID properties (Atomicity, Consistency, Isolation, Durability).

Stored Procedure:

A stored procedure is a precompiled SQL statement that can be executed multiple times. It's stored in the database and can accept parameters for flexibility.

View:

A view is a virtual table that consists of data from one or more tables. Views are created to simplify complex queries, enhance data security, and abstract the underlying table structure.

Triggers:

Triggers are database objects that automatically execute in response to specific events, such as data changes in a table. They are used for enforcing business rules and maintaining data integrity.

Relational Database Management System (RDBMS):

An RDBMS is a software system that manages relational databases. MySQL is an example of an RDBMS that uses structured data organized in tables.

Backup and Recovery:

Backup involves making copies of the database to safeguard data against loss or corruption. Recovery is the process of restoring the database to a previous state using backup copies in case of data loss.

These fundamental database terms provide a foundation for working with MySQL databases and understanding how data is organized and managed within the system.

1.7 Exercise

Exercise 1 – MCQ

Q 1. Who originally developed the first version of MySQL?

A) Microsoft Corporation

B) Oracle Corporation

C) Sybase and Microsoft (jointly)

D) IBM Corporation

Q 2. Which step follows the download of the MySQL installation package when installing MySQL on a Windows system?

A) Configuration

B) Testing

C) Licensing

D) Running the installer

Exercise 2 – True/ False

Q 1. After downloading the MySQL installation package, the next step in installing MySQL on a Windows system is Licensing."

Q 2. After downloading the MySQL installation package, the next step in installing MySQL on a Windows system is "Configuration."

Exercise 3 – Fill in the blanks

Q 1. SQL Server 4.2 marked Microsoft's full control over MySQL's development, and it introduced support for the 32-bit operating system ___________.

Q 2. In the installation of MySQL on a Windows system, the step that follows the download of the MySQL installation package is "Running the ________."

Exercise 4 – One word answer

Q 1. What component of MySQL handles client connections and authentication?

Q 2. What license is typically associated with MySQL Community Edition?

Exercise 5 – Small answer

Q 1. What is the primary difference between MySQL Community Edition and MySQL Enterprise Edition?

Q 2. What does the SQL layer in MySQL handle primarily?

Exercise 6 – Long answer

Q 1. Explain the differences between MySQL Community Edition and MySQL Enterprise Edition, highlighting their respective features, licensing models, and target users.

Q 2. Describe the licensing options for MySQL, including the difference between MySQL Community Edition and MySQL Enterprise Edition. Also, outline the steps involved in the installation of MySQL on a Windows system.

Answer

Exercise 1

Answer 1: C) 2: D)

Exercise 2

Answer 1: False 2: True.

Exercise 3

Answer 1: Windows NT 2: Installer

Exercise 4

Answer 1: Connection 2: GPL

ONLINE RESOURCES

Practice Paper

Link: https://forms.gle/2FgU4Kcd5zKVXeDT8

QR Code:

Video Content:

Link: https://www.youtube.com/playlist?list=PLzlh_31VWEFob91YvVOqYVtTg2-OgJMQ5

QR Code:

Chapter 2: Getting Started with SQL

2.1 SQL Basics

SQL is a powerful language used for managing and manipulating relational databases. It enables users to interact with databases to perform tasks such as retrieving data, adding new data, updating existing data, and deleting data. Here are the fundamental concepts and components of SQL:

Relational Databases:

SQL is primarily designed for managing relational databases. A relational database organizes data into tables (also known as relations), where each table consists of rows (records) and columns (attributes).

SQL Statements:

SQL consists of various statements for performing different database operations. The most common types of SQL statements include:

SELECT: Used to retrieve data from one or more tables.
INSERT: Adds new data rows to a table.
UPDATE: Modifies existing data in a table.
DELETE: Removes data rows from a table.
CREATE: Creates a new database, table, or other database object.
ALTER: Modifies the structure of an existing database object.
DROP: Deletes a database object (e.g., table, index).

SQL Syntax:

SQL statements follow a specific syntax. They typically consist of clauses and keywords arranged in a specific order. For example, a basic SELECT statement looks like this:

```
SELECT column1, column2
FROM table_name
WHERE condition;
```

SELECT: Specifies the columns to retrieve.
FROM: Specifies the table(s) from which to retrieve data.
WHERE (optional): Filters rows based on a specified condition.

Tables and Fields:

In SQL, data is stored in tables. Each table is defined by a set of fields (columns) and contains rows (records) representing individual data entries. Fields have data types that define the kind of data they can hold (e.g., integer, text, date).

Primary Keys:

A primary key is a unique identifier for each row in a table. It ensures data integrity by preventing duplicate records. Primary keys are often used for referencing records from other tables (foreign keys).

Foreign Keys:

A foreign key is a field in one table that references the primary key of another table. It establishes relationships between tables, enabling data consistency and integrity.

Indexes:

Indexes improve query performance by providing fast access to specific data. They work like the index in a book, allowing SQL to quickly locate the required information.

Constraints:

Constraints are rules applied to tables to maintain data integrity. Common constraints include NOT NULL (ensuring a field cannot be empty) and UNIQUE (ensuring unique values in a field).

SQL Operators:

SQL includes operators like = (equal), != (not equal), > (greater than), < (less than), and others for performing comparisons and calculations in queries.

SQL Functions:

SQL provides various built-in functions for data manipulation, including mathematical functions (e.g., SUM, AVG), string functions (e.g., CONCAT, LENGTH), and date functions (e.g., DATEFORMAT, DATEADD).

SQL Joins:

SQL allows you to combine data from multiple tables using JOIN operations. Common types of joins include INNER JOIN, LEFT JOIN, and RIGHT JOIN.

Transactions:

SQL supports transactions, which are sequences of one or more SQL statements treated as a single unit of work. Transactions ensure data consistency by allowing you to commit or roll back changes.

SQL Management Tools:

To work with SQL databases, you can use various management tools like SQL Server Management Studio (SSMS) for Microsoft SQL Server, MySQL Workbench for MySQL, and PostgreSQL pgAdmin for PostgreSQL.

Understanding these SQL basics is essential for interacting with relational databases and performing various data-related tasks effectively. SQL is a versatile language that plays a crucial role in data management and retrieval in a wide range of applications.

2.2 SQL Data Types

In Microsoft SQL Server, data types define the kind of data that can be stored in a database column. SQL Server provides a variety of data types to accommodate different types of data, such as integers, text, dates, and more. Let's explore the SQL data types in SQL Server in detail:

Numeric Data Types:

These data types are used for storing numeric values, including integers and decimals.
Common numeric data types include:
INT: Represents a 32-bit signed integer.
BIGINT: Stores a 64-bit signed integer.
SMALLINT: Holds a 16-bit signed integer.
DECIMAL or NUMERIC: Used for fixed-point numbers with a specified precision and scale.
FLOAT: Stores approximate numeric values with a floating-point precision.

Character String Data Types:

These data types are used for storing character strings and textual data.
Common character string data types include:
CHAR(n): Fixed-length character string with a specified length n.
VARCHAR(n): Variable-length character string with a maximum length of n.
TEXT: Stores large blocks of text data, suitable for long documents.

Binary Data Types:

These data types are used for storing binary data, such as images or files.
Common binary data types include:
BINARY(n): Fixed-length binary data with a specified length n.
VARBINARY(n): Variable-length binary data with a maximum length of n.
IMAGE: Stores large binary data, such as images or multimedia files.

Date and Time Data Types:

These data types are used for storing date and time values.
Common date and time data types include:
DATE: Stores date values only.
TIME: Stores time values.
DATETIME or DATETIME2: Stores date and time values with fractional seconds precision.
SMALLDATETIME: Stores date and time values with reduced precision for storage efficiency.

Boolean Data Type:

SQL Server does not have a dedicated Boolean data type. Instead, it uses BIT, which can represent 0 (false), 1 (true), or NULL (unknown).

Uniqueidentifier Data Type:

UNIQUEIDENTIFIER stores a globally unique identifier (GUID). It is often used as a primary key for replication and distributed systems.

Other Specialized Data Types:

SQL Server provides several specialized data types for specific purposes, including:
XML: Stores XML data.
SQL_VARIANT: Stores values of different data types.
GEOMETRY and GEOGRAPHY: Used for spatial data, such as geographic coordinates.
HIERARCHYID: Stores hierarchical data.
TIMESTAMP (deprecated): Used for versioning and tracking changes.

User-Defined Data Types (UDTs):

SQL Server allows you to create custom data types based on existing data types. These user-defined data types can simplify database design and enforce data consistency.

Choosing the appropriate data type is essential for efficient storage and data integrity. It's important to consider factors like data size, precision, and the nature of the data when selecting a data type for a column in your database schema. Proper data type selection can help optimize database performance and ensure data accuracy.

2.3 Creating and Managing Databases

Creating and managing databases in Microsoft SQL Server is a fundamental aspect of database administration. Here, we'll explain the process of creating and managing databases in SQL Server:

Creating a Database:

To create a new database in SQL Server, you can use SQL Server Management Studio (SSMS) or write SQL statements. Here's how to create a database using SSMS:
Open SQL Server Management Studio.
Connect to your SQL Server instance.
In the Object Explorer, right-click on "Databases."
Select "New Database."
Provide a name for your database.
Configure the database settings, such as the file locations, initial size, and growth options.
Click "OK" to create the database.
If you prefer using SQL statements, you can use the CREATE DATABASE command:

```
CREATE DATABASE YourDatabaseName;
```

Managing Database Properties:

After creating a database, you can manage its properties to fine-tune its behavior. Some important properties include:

Filegroups: SQL Server allows you to organize database files into filegroups. You can create and manage filegroups to optimize data storage and backups.

Collation: Specify the collation for the database, which determines how string comparisons and sorting are performed.

Recovery Model: Choose the appropriate recovery model based on your backup and recovery requirements. Options include Full, Simple, and Bulk-Logged.

Compatibility Level: Set the compatibility level to control how the database behaves with regard to older SQL Server versions.

Creating Tables:

Once the database is created, you can create tables to store data. Use the CREATE TABLE statement to define the table's structure, including column names, data types, constraints, and indexes.

```
CREATE TABLE Employees (
  EmployeeID INT PRIMARY KEY,
  FirstName NVARCHAR(50),
  LastName NVARCHAR(50),
  HireDate DATE
);
```

Managing Data:

You can insert, update, and delete data in your tables using SQL statements. For example:

INSERT INTO is used to add new rows of data.

UPDATE is used to modify existing data.

DELETE is used to remove data.

```
INSERT INTO Employees (EmployeeID, FirstName, LastName, HireDate)
VALUES (1, 'John', 'Doe', '2022-01-15');

UPDATE Employees
SET FirstName = 'Jane'
WHERE EmployeeID = 1;

DELETE FROM Employees
WHERE EmployeeID = 1;
```

Indexing:

To optimize query performance, you can create indexes on columns that are frequently used in search and join operations. SQL Server provides different types of indexes, including clustered and non-clustered indexes.

Backup and Restore:

Regularly back up your databases to prevent data loss. SQL Server offers various backup and restore options. You can use SSMS or SQL statements like BACKUP DATABASE and RESTORE DATABASE to manage backups.

Security and Permissions:

SQL Server allows you to control access to your database by setting permissions and roles. You can create logins, users, and assign specific permissions to control who can view, modify, or administer the database.

Maintenance Plans:

SQL Server includes tools for creating maintenance plans to automate tasks like backups, index rebuilds, and database consistency checks.

Monitoring and Optimization:

Use SQL Server's built-in tools and performance monitoring features to identify and resolve performance issues. SQL Profiler, Query Store, and Dynamic Management Views (DMVs) are valuable resources for optimization.

Dropping Databases:

To remove a database, you can use the `DROP DATABASE` statement:

DROP DATABASE YourDatabaseName;

Be cautious when dropping databases, as this action permanently deletes all data and objects associated with the database. Managing databases in SQL Server is a critical skill for database administrators and developers. Properly designing and maintaining databases ensures data integrity, security, and optimal performance for your applications and systems.

2.4 MySQL Command-Line Client

Introduction to MySQL Command-Line Client: The MySQL Command-Line Client is a powerful and versatile tool that allows users to interact with MySQL databases through a command-line interface. It is a text-based application that enables users to manage and manipulate MySQL databases, issue SQL queries, and perform various database-related tasks using a series of commands.

The primary purpose of the MySQL Command-Line Client is to provide database administrators, developers, and users with a straightforward and efficient means of working with MySQL databases. Some of the key functionalities and use cases of the MySQL Command-Line Client include:

Running SQL Queries: Users can execute SQL statements to retrieve, insert, update, and delete data in MySQL databases. This is especially useful for querying and manipulating data stored in the database.

Database Management: The client allows for the creation, modification, and deletion of databases, tables, and other database objects.

User and Privilege Management: Administrators can use the client to create and manage user accounts, assign privileges, and control access to the database.

Data Import and Export: It provides utilities like **mysqldump** for backing up databases and exporting data, and **mysql** for importing data into databases. This is crucial for data migration and backup purposes.

Scripting and Automation: Users can write scripts or batch files to automate repetitive database tasks or perform more complex operations.

Troubleshooting and Debugging: The command-line client is a valuable tool for diagnosing and troubleshooting issues within the database, as it provides detailed error messages and feedback.

In summary, the MySQL Command-Line Client is an essential component for anyone working with MySQL databases. It provides a direct and efficient way to manage and interact with MySQL data, making it a preferred choice for many database administrators and developers.

Installing MySQL Command-Line Client: Installing the MySQL Command-Line Client is a crucial step for anyone looking to work with MySQL databases from the command line. Below, I'll explain how to download and install the MySQL Command-Line Client on different operating systems:

On Windows:

Visit the MySQL Community Downloads page on the MySQL website.

Choose the appropriate MySQL Community Server edition for Windows and click on the "Download" button.

Select the "MySQL Installer for Windows" option. This installer includes the MySQL Command-Line Client.

Follow the installation wizard, which will guide you through the installation process.

During installation, you can choose to install specific MySQL components, including the Command-Line Client.

Once the installation is complete, you can access the MySQL Command-Line Client from the Windows Command Prompt or MySQL Command Line Client shortcut.

On macOS:

You can install the MySQL Command-Line Client on macOS using the Homebrew package manager. If you don't have Homebrew installed, follow their installation instructions first.

Open a terminal and run the following command to install the MySQL Command-Line Client:

```
brew install mysql-client
```

After installation, you can access the MySQL Command-Line Client by running the **mysql** command in your terminal.

On Linux (Ubuntu/Debian):

Use the package manager to install the MySQL Command-Line Client. Open a terminal and run the following command:

```
sudo apt-get update
sudo apt-get install mysql-client
```

After installation, you can access the MySQL Command-Line Client by running the **mysql** command in your terminal.

On Linux (CentOS/Fedora):

Use the package manager to install the MySQL Command-Line Client. Open a terminal and run the following command:

```
sudo yum install mysql
```

After installation, you can access the MySQL Command-Line Client by running the **mysql** command in your terminal.

Once you've completed the installation on your preferred operating system, you'll have access to the MySQL Command-Line Client, allowing you to start interacting with MySQL databases from the command line.

Navigate to the official **https://dev.mysql.com/downloads/mysql/**

Connecting to a MySQL Database: This command invokes **mysql** without specifying any explicit connection parameters:

mysql

Because there are no parameter options, the default values apply:

The default host name is localhost. On Unix, this has a special meaning, as described later.

The default user name is ODBC on Windows or your Unix login name on Unix.

No password is sent because neither --password nor -p is given.

For **mysql**, the first nonoption argument is taken as the name of the default database. Because there is no such argument, **mysql** selects no default database.

To specify the host name and user name explicitly, as well as a password, supply appropriate options on the command line. To select a default database, add a database-name argument. Examples:

mysql --host=localhost --user=myname --password=*password* mydb

mysql -h localhost -u myname -p*password* mydb

For password options, the password value is optional:

If you use a --password or -p option and specify a password value, there must be *no space* between --password= or -p and the password following it.

If you use --password or -p but do not specify a password value, the client program prompts you to enter the password. The password is not displayed as you enter it. This is more secure than giving the password on the command line, which might enable other users on your system to see the password line by executing a command such as **ps**.

To explicitly specify that there is no password and that the client program should not prompt for one, use the --skip-password option.

s just mentioned, including the password value on the command line is a security risk. To avoid this risk, specify the --password or -p option without any following password value:

mysql --host=localhost --user=myname --password mydb

mysql -h localhost -u myname -p mydb

When the --password or -p option is given with no password value, the client program prints a prompt and waits for you to enter the password. (In these examples, mydb is *not* interpreted as a password because it is separated from the preceding password option by a space.)

How to connect to MySQL

There are two main ways you can connect to a MySQL database:

MySQL beginners may feel more comfortable with graphical user interface (GUI) tools like **MySQL Workbench** (for Windows and Mac) or **Sequel Ace** (only for Mac). These visual tools make it easier for new users to find the options they're looking for.

If you're more comfortable with MySQL, you can use command options via **Command Line** (for Windows) or **Terminal** (for Mac). This option will be faster and give you more control if you know what you're doing.

How to connect using MySQL Workbench

MySQL Workbench is a good choice for Windows users who are new to MySQL. It might also be a solid option if you would use its bonus functionalities like designing databases or accessing its visual performance dashboard.

If you want to use MySQL Workbench to connect to a database, follow these steps to download the software.

Navigate to the official MySQL Workbench download page.

Select your operating system.

Select your OS version.

Click Download next to DMG Archive for Mac or Go to Download Page next to MySQL Installer MSI for Windows.

On the next screen, click No thanks, just start my download.

Follow your computer's guided instructions for downloading.

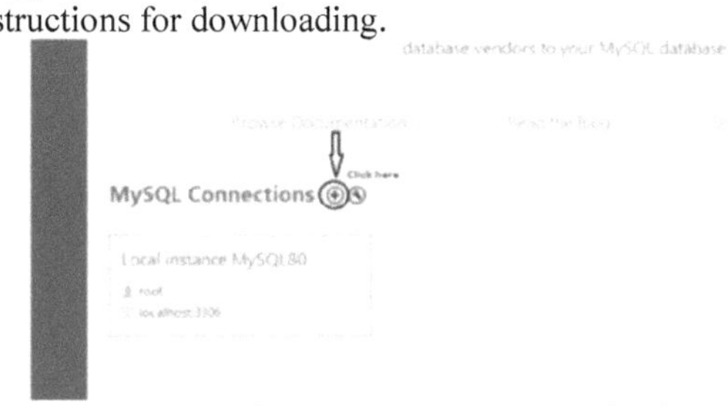

Once you've downloaded the software, you can use it to connect to MySQL databases with these steps.

Open MySQL Workbench.

Click the + button next to MySQL connections.

In the pop-up window, type in what you'd like to call the connection in *Connection Name*. Then type in the *Hostname*, *Port*, *Username*, and *Password* (if there is one) for the database you want to connect to.

Click **Test connection** if you're not 100% positive you have the right information.

You'll get a pop-up box like this if you're successful. Click **OK**.

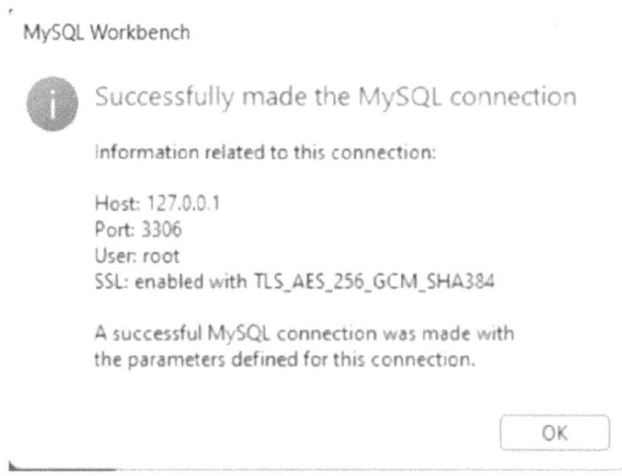

Click **OK** again on the previous window.

You'll now see the connection listed under MySQL Connections. Click on your new connection.

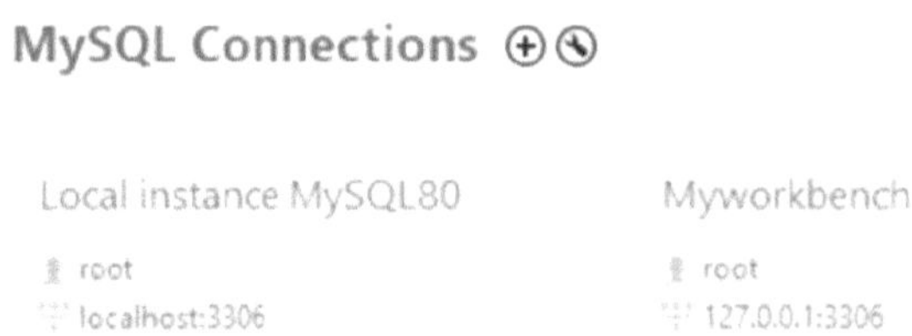

If your database requires a password, you'll have to enter it before your connection loads. Once you've entered the password, you'll be taken to the database.

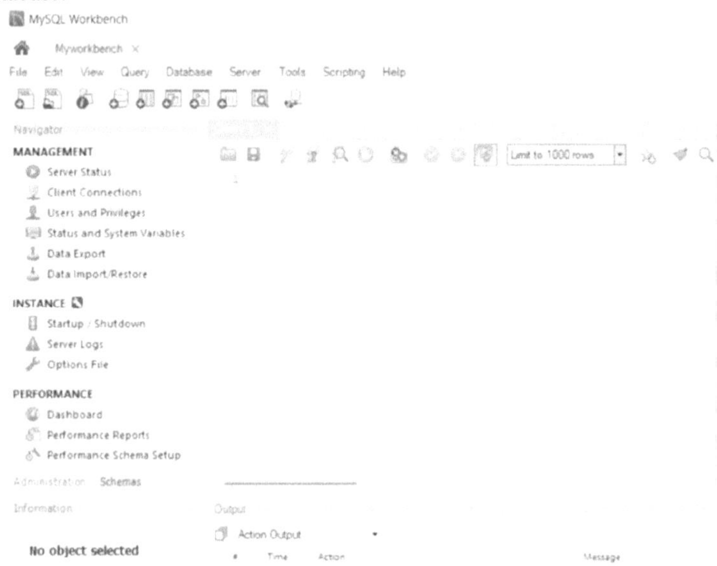

Executing SQL Queries: Executing SQL queries in MySQL, including commonly used statements like SELECT, INSERT, UPDATE, and DELETE, can be done using the MySQL Command-Line Client. Below, I'll explain how to execute these SQL queries using the command-line client:

SELECT Statements:

To retrieve data from a MySQL database using SELECT statements:

Open a terminal or command prompt.

Log in to MySQL with the **mysql** command and your username and password:

mysql -u your_username -p

You'll be prompted to enter your password.

Choose the database you want to query using the **USE** statement:

USE your_database_name;

Execute your SELECT query. For example, to select all records from a table:

SELECT * FROM your_table_name;

Replace "your_table_name" with the actual table name.

Press Enter to see the results.

INSERT Statements:
To insert data into a MySQL database using INSERT statements:
After logging in to MySQL, select the database using the **USE** statement as described above.
Execute your INSERT query. For example, to insert a new record into a table:
INSERT INTO your_table_name (column1, column2, ...) VALUES (value1, value2, ...);
Replace "your_table_name" with the table name, and specify the column names and values to insert.
Press Enter to execute the query.
UPDATE Statements:
To update data in a MySQL database using UPDATE statements:
After logging in to MySQL, select the database using the **USE** statement.
Execute your UPDATE query. For example, to update data in a table:
UPDATE your_table_name SET column1 = new_value1, column2 = new_value2 WHERE some_condition;
Replace "your_table_name" with the table name, specify the columns to update and their new values, and define the condition to identify the rows to update.
Press Enter to execute the query.
DELETE Statements:
To delete data from a MySQL database using DELETE statements:
After logging in to MySQL, select the database using the **USE** statement.
Execute your DELETE query. For example, to delete specific records from a table:
DELETE FROM your_table_name WHERE some_condition;
Replace "your_table_name" with the table name, and specify the condition to identify the rows to delete.
Press Enter to execute the query.
You can also execute other SQL statements using a similar approach, such as CREATE, ALTER, and DROP statements for database and table management, and more complex queries involving JOINs, GROUP BY, and ORDER BY clauses. The MySQL Command-Line Client is a powerful tool for interacting with your database through the command line, offering flexibility and control over your SQL operations.
Executing SQL Queries in the MySQL Command-Line Client:
Open your MySQL Command-Line Client and log in to your MySQL server.
Select the appropriate database using the **USE** statement:

USE your_database_name;

Execute the SQL query directly in the command-line client by typing or pasting the query and pressing Enter.
The results of SELECT queries will be displayed on the screen, showing the data retrieved. For INSERT, UPDATE, and DELETE queries, you will receive a confirmation message indicating the number of affected rows.
Remember to be cautious when executing UPDATE and DELETE queries, as they can modify or remove data from your database, and there's no automatic undo operation. It's a good practice to test your queries with SELECT statements first to ensure you are targeting the right data.

2.5 Creating a Database and Creating Tables

Creating a database and tables in MySQL involves defining the structure and organization of your data. Here, I'll explain how to create a database and then create tables within that database in MySQL, both through the command-line interface and SQL statements.
Creating a Database:
Command-Line Method:
Open a terminal or command prompt.
Log in to MySQL with the **mysql** command and your MySQL username and password:

mysql -u your_username -p

You'll be prompted to enter your password.
To create a new database, use the **CREATE DATABASE** statement. Replace "your_database_name" with your desired database name:

CREATE DATABASE your_database_name;

To switch to the newly created database, use the **USE** statement:

USE your_database_name;

SQL Statement Method: You can also create a database using SQL statements without entering the MySQL command-line interface. For this, you can use a MySQL client like phpMyAdmin or execute SQL statements in a script. Here's the SQL statement to create a database:

```
CREATE DATABASE your_database_name;
```

Creating Tables:

Once you have a database, you can create tables to structure your data.

Command-Line Method:

Still in the MySQL command-line client, make sure you've selected the correct database using the **USE** statement (as shown in the command-line method for creating a database).

To create a table, use the **CREATE TABLE** statement. Replace "your_table_name" with the name of your table, and define the columns and their data types:

```
CREATE TABLE your_table_name (
column1_name data_type,
column2_name data_type,
...,
columnN_name data_type
);
```

For example, to create a simple "users" table:

```
CREATE TABLE users (
id INT AUTO_INCREMENT PRIMARY KEY,
username VARCHAR(50) NOT NULL,
email VARCHAR(100) NOT NULL,
created_at TIMESTAMP DEFAULT CURRENT_TIMESTAMP
);
```

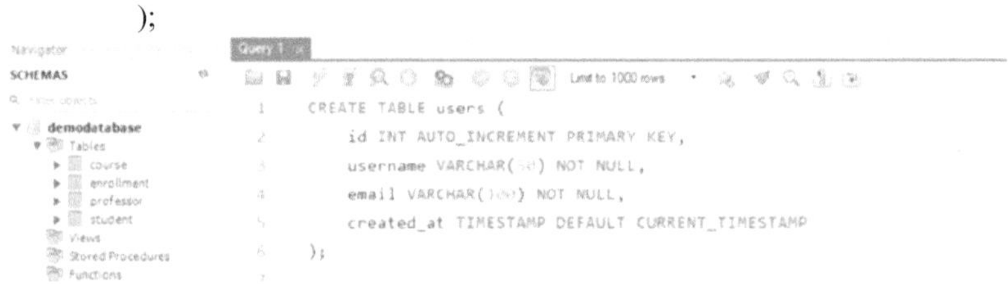

Table users is created

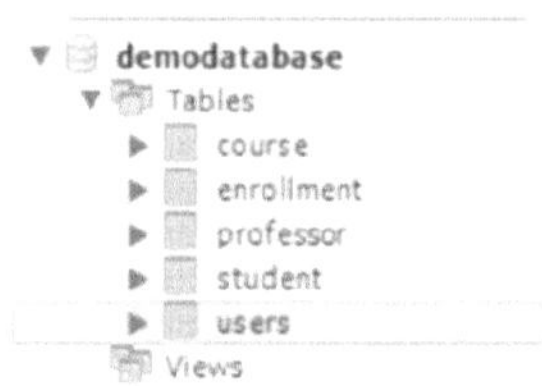

SQL Statement Method: You can also create tables using SQL statements outside the MySQL command-line client. Here's the SQL statement to create a table:

```
CREATE TABLE your_table_name (
column1_name data_type,
column2_name data_type,
...,
columnN_name data_type
);
```

In the example above, "your_table_name" is the name of your table, and you define the table's columns along with their data types.

Remember that this is a simplified example. In practice, you may need to define constraints, such as primary keys, foreign keys, and indexes, depending on your specific requirements.

After creating a table, you can start inserting data into it, querying it, and performing other database operations to manage and retrieve your data effectively.

Selecting, Creating, Dropping, and Altering Databases

In MySQL Workbench, a popular graphical user interface tool for MySQL, you can perform various database-related tasks, including selecting, creating, dropping, and altering databases. Here's a step-by-step guide on how to accomplish these tasks in MySQL Workbench:

Selecting a Database:

Open MySQL Workbench and connect to your MySQL server.

Once connected, you should see a list of available databases in the Navigator panel on the left-hand side. If the Navigator panel is not visible, you can enable it from the "View" menu.

To select a database, simply click on the database name in the Navigator panel. This action will set the selected database as the active database for your current session.

Creating a Database:

In MySQL Workbench, you can create a new database by following these steps:

In the Navigator panel, right-click on the "Databases" folder or the schema where you want to create the new database.

Choose "Create Schema..." or "Create Database..." from the context menu, depending on your MySQL version.

A dialog box will appear. Enter the name of the new database in the "Schema Name" or "Database Name" field.

You can configure other settings, such as the default character set and collation.

Click the "Apply" button to create the database.

The new database should now appear in the Navigator panel.

Dropping a Database:

Be extremely careful when dropping a database because this action permanently deletes all the data within it.

To drop a database in MySQL Workbench, follow these steps:

In the Navigator panel, locate the database you want to delete.

Right-click on the database name and select "Drop Schema..." or "Drop Database..." from the context menu, depending on your MySQL version.

A confirmation dialog will appear, asking if you are sure you want to delete the database.

Confirm the action, and MySQL Workbench will drop the database.

Exploring Databases and Tables with SHOW and mysqlshow

You can explore databases and tables in MySQL using the **SHOW** statement and the **mysqlshow** command. These tools provide information about the databases and tables available in your MySQL server. Here's how to use them:

Using the SHOW Statement:

The **SHOW** statement is a SQL command that allows you to retrieve information about databases, tables, and other objects within your MySQL server. It is typically used within the MySQL command-line client or in SQL scripts. Here are some common use cases:

To list all the databases available in your MySQL server:

```
SHOW DATABASES;
```

To show the tables within a specific database:

```
SHOW TABLES IN your_database_name;
```

To display the structure of a table, including its columns:

```
SHOW COLUMNS FROM your_table_name;
```

To retrieve information about a table's indexes:

```
SHOW INDEX FROM your_table_name;
```

To list the privileges granted to a specific user or role:

```
SHOW GRANTS FOR 'your_username'@'your_host';
```

Using the mysqlshow Command:

The **mysqlshow** command is a command-line utility that provides a convenient way to view information about databases and tables. It can be executed in your terminal or command prompt. Here's how to use it:

To list all the databases available in your MySQL server:

```
mysqlshow -u your_username -p
```

You will be prompted to enter your MySQL password.

To show the tables within a specific database:

```
mysqlshow -u your_username -p your_database_name
```

To display information about a specific table within a database:

```
mysqlshow -u your_username -p your_database_name your_table_name
```

To list all tables and their details in a specific database:

```
mysqlshow -u your_username -p -i your_database_name
```

The **-i** option provides more detailed information about the tables, including their indexes.

The **mysqlshow** command provides a quick overview of the structure and status of your databases and tables. It's a useful tool for administrators and developers who want to gather information about their MySQL server without having to log in to the MySQL command-line client.
Both the **SHOW** statement and the **mysqlshow** command are essential tools for exploring your MySQL databases and tables, whether you need a high-level view of your database structure or detailed information about specific tables and their columns.

2.7 Exercise

Exercise 1 – MCQ

Q 1. Which of the following statements is true about SQL?
A) SQL stands for Structured Programming Language.
B) SQL is a programming language used for creating websites.
C) SQL is a domain-specific language for managing and querying relational databases.
D) SQL is primarily used for building mobile applications.
Q 2. When creating a table in SQL, which keyword is used to specify a column as an auto-incrementing, unique identifier?
A) PRIMARY KEY
B) INDEX
C) UNIQUE
D) AUTO_INCREMENT

Exercise 2 – True/ False

Q 1. SQL stands for Structured Query Language, and it is used to manage and manipulate data stored in relational databases.
Q 2. The MySQL Command-Line Client is a graphical user interface (GUI) tool for interacting with MySQL databases.

Exercise 3 – One word answer

Q 1. What does SQL stand for?
Q 2. Which SQL command is used to retrieve data from a database?

Exercise 4 – Small answer

Q 1. What is SQL used for?
Q 2. How do you create a new database using MySQL Command-Line Client?

Exercise 5 – Long answer

Q 1. What are the fundamental concepts and steps to get started with SQL, including an overview of SQL basics, data types, and creating and managing databases?
Q 2. How can you use the MySQL Command-Line Client to interact with a MySQL database, including connecting, executing queries, and managing data?

Answer

Exercise 1
Answer 1: C), 2: D)
Exercise 2
Answer 1: True, 2: False.
Exercise 3
Answer 1: Structured Query Language, 2: SELECT.

ONLINE RESOURCES

Practice Paper
Link: https://forms.gle/sQNhGSwPQxSiakSE8
QR Code:

Video Content:
Link: https://www.youtube.com/playlist?list=PLzlh_31VWEFrxCQZ9ZXZ7AllrLd7KhCks
QR Code:

Chapter 3: Querying and Data Manipulation

3.1 SELECT Statements

In MySQL, the SELECT statement is a fundamental SQL command used to retrieve data from one or more tables. It allows you to specify the columns you want to retrieve, apply filters, sort the results, and more. Here's an overview of the SELECT statement in MySQL:

Basic SELECT Syntax:

```
SELECT column1, column2, ...
FROM table_name;
```

Retrieving All Columns:

```
SELECT *
FROM employees;
```

Filtering Rows with WHERE Clause:

```
SELECT column1, column2, ...
FROM table_name
WHERE condition;
```

Example:

```
SELECT product_name, price
FROM products
WHERE price > 50;
```

Sorting Results with ORDER BY Clause:

```
SELECT column1, column2, ...
FROM table_name
ORDER BY column_to_sort [ASC|DESC];
```

Using Aliases:

```
SELECT first_name AS "First Name", last_name AS "Last Name"
FROM employees;
```

Removing Duplicate Rows with DISTINCT:

```
SELECT DISTINCT department_id
FROM employees;
```

Combining Columns:

```
SELECT first_name || ' ' || last_name AS "Full Name"
FROM employees;
```

Combining Filtering and Sorting:

You can use the WHERE and ORDER BY clauses in a single query to retrieve and order data based on specific criteria.

```
SELECT column1, column2, ...
FROM table_name
WHERE condition
ORDER BY column_to_sort [ASC|DESC];
```

Limiting Rows with LIMIT (MySQL-specific):

```
SELECT first_name, last_name
FROM employees
LIMIT 5;
```

Aggregate Functions:

MySQL supports various aggregate functions, such as SUM, AVG, COUNT, MIN, and MAX, for summarizing and calculating data.

```
SELECT department_id, AVG(salary) AS "Average Salary"
FROM employees
GROUP BY department_id;
```

The SELECT statement in MySQL is a versatile tool for retrieving and manipulating data. By combining various clauses, functions, and operators, you can tailor your queries to meet specific data retrieval and analysis requirements. Understanding these SQL concepts is essential for working effectively with MySQL databases.

3.2 Filtering and Sorting Data

Filtering and sorting data are fundamental operations when working with databases, and MySQL provides powerful capabilities to perform these tasks. Here's an overview of how to filter and sort data in MySQL:

Filtering Data with the `WHERE` Clause:

The `WHERE` clause is used to filter rows based on specified conditions.

```
SELECT column1, column2, ...
FROM table_name
WHERE condition;
```

column1, column2, ...: Columns to retrieve.
Table_name: Name of the table.
Condition: The condition that rows must satisfy.
Example:

```
SELECT product_name, price
FROM products
WHERE price > 50;
```

Sorting Data with the `ORDER BY` Clause:

The `ORDER BY` clause is used to sort the result set based on one or more columns.

```
SELECT column1, mn2, ...
FROM table_name
ORDER BY column_to_sort [ASC|DESC];
```

column_to_sort: The column by which to sort the result.
ASC: Ascending order (default).
DESC: Descending order.
Example:

```
SELECT employee_id, last_name, hire_date
FROM employees
ORDER BY hire_date DESC;
```

Combining Filtering and Sorting:

You can use both the `WHERE` and `ORDER BY` clauses in a single query to retrieve and order data based on specific criteria.

```
SELECT column1, column2, ...
FROM table_name
WHERE condition
ORDER BY column_to_sort [ASC|DESC];
```

Example:

```
SELECT first_name, last_name, hire_date
FROM employees
WHERE department_id = 30
ORDER BY hire_date;
```

Removing Duplicate Rows with `DISTINCT`:

The `DISTINCT` keyword ensures that only unique values are retrieved.

```
SELECT DISTINCT department_id
FROM employees;
```

3.3 Joins and Subqueries

Joins and subqueries are advanced SQL techniques that allow you to retrieve and manipulate data from multiple tables and apply complex conditions. MySQL provides robust support for both joins and subqueries. Here's a detailed overview of how to use joins and subqueries effectively in MySQL:

Joins:

Joins are used to combine rows from two or more tables based on related columns. There are various types of joins in MySQL:

INNER JOIN: An inner join returns only the rows that have matching values in both tables.

```
SELECT customers.customer_name, orders.order_date
FROM customers
INNER JOIN orders ON customers.customer_id = orders.customer_id;
```

LEFT JOIN (or LEFT OUTER JOIN):

A left join returns all rows from the left table and the matched rows from the right table. If there is no match, NULL values are returned for the right table.

```
SELECT employees.first_name, departments.department_name
FROM employees
LEFT JOIN departments ON employees.department_id = departments.department_id;
```

RIGHT JOIN (or RIGHT OUTER JOIN):

A right join returns all rows from the right table and the matched rows from the left table. If there is no match, NULL values are returned for the left table.

```
SELECT products.product_name, order_details.quantity
FROM products
RIGHT JOIN order_details ON products.product_id = order_details.product_id;
```

FULL OUTER JOIN:

A full outer join returns all rows from both tables. If there is no match, NULL values are returned for the columns from the non-matching table.

```
SELECT customers.customer_name, orders.order_id
FROM customers
FULL OUTER JOIN orders ON customers.customer_id = orders.customer_id;
```

Subqueries:

Subqueries, also known as nested queries or inner queries, are queries embedded within another SQL statement. They can be used in various parts of a SQL statement, such as the SELECT, FROM, WHERE, and HAVING clauses.

Scalar Subquery:

A scalar subquery returns a single value and can be used in any place where a single value is expected.

```
SELECT product_name, price
FROM products
WHERE price > (SELECT AVG(price) FROM products);
```

Correlated Subquery:

A correlated subquery refers to columns from the outer query and is evaluated once for each row processed by the outer query.

```
SELECT employee_name, salary
FROM employees e
WHERE salary > (SELECT AVG(salary) FROM employees WHERE department_id = e.department_id);
```

Subquery in the FROM Clause (Derived Table):

You can use a subquery in the FROM clause to create a derived table, which can be treated like a regular table in the outer query.

```
SELECT department_name, AVG(salary) AS avg_salary
FROM (SELECT * FROM employees WHERE salary > 50000) filtered_employees
GROUP BY department_name;
```

Subquery in the WHERE Clause:

Subqueries in the WHERE clause are often used to filter rows based on values from another table.

```
SELECT customer_name
FROM customers
WHERE customer_id IN (SELECT customer_id FROM orders WHERE order_date >= TO_DATE('2022-02-01', 'YYYY-MM-DD'));
```

Joins and subqueries are powerful tools in MySQL for querying and retrieving data from complex database structures. They allow you to extract meaningful information from related tables, apply conditional logic, and perform advanced data manipulation. Understanding when and how to use joins and subqueries is crucial for effective SQL query writing.

3.4 Inserting, Updating, and Deleting Data

In MySQL, you can perform various operations to manipulate data in tables, including inserting new records, updating existing records, and deleting records. These operations are crucial for maintaining the integrity and accuracy of your database. Here's how to perform these tasks:

Inserting Data:

The INSERT statement is used to add new records (rows) to a table. There are two primary ways to insert data into a table:

Inserting Data into Specific Columns:

```
INSERT INTO table_name (column1, column2, ...)
VALUES (value1, value2, ...);
```

table_name: Name of the table.
Column1, column2, …: Names of the columns you want to insert data into.
Value1, value2, …: Values you want to insert into the specified columns.
Examples:
INSERT INTO customers (customer_name, email, phone)
VALUES ('John Smith', 'john@example.com', '555-123-4567');

Inserting Data into All Columns:
If you want to insert data into all columns of a table, you can omit the column list.
INSERT INTO table_name
VALUES (value1, value2, …);
Examples:
INSERT INTO employees
VALUES (101, 'Alice', 'Johnson', '2020-03-15', 'HR', 45000);

Updating Data:
The UPDATE statement is used to modify existing records in a table.
UPDATE table_name
SET column1 = new_value1, column2 = new_value2, …
WHERE condition;

table_name: Name of the table.
Column1, column2, …: Columns you want to update.
New_value1, new_value2, …: New values you want to set for the specified columns.
Condition: Condition that determines which rows to update.
Examples:
UPDATE products
SET price = 25.99
WHERE product_id = 101;

Deleting Data:
The DELETE statement is used to remove records from a table.
DELETE FROM table_name
WHERE condition;
table_name: Name of the table.
Condition: Condition that specifies which rows to delete.
Example:
DELETE FROM customers
WHERE customer_id = 201;
Note: Be cautious when using the DELETE statement, as it permanently removes data from the table.
Batch Operations:
You can perform batch operations to insert, update, or delete multiple records at once by using appropriate conditions or specifying multiple sets of values in the INSERT statement.
These data manipulation operations are essential for maintaining data consistency and making changes to your MySQL database. Always ensure that you have proper backups and thoroughly test your SQL statements before performing data manipulation operations, especially updates and deletes, to avoid unintended data loss or corruption.

3.5 Advanced Querying
Advanced querying in SQL involves using more complex SQL statements and techniques to retrieve, manipulate, and analyse data from a database. Advanced queries are often required when dealing with real-world data and complex relationships. Here are some advanced querying topics and techniques:
JOIN Operations:
INNER JOIN: Combines rows from two or more tables based on a related column between them.
LEFT JOIN (or LEFT OUTER JOIN): Retrieves all rows from the left table and matching rows from the right table.
RIGHT JOIN (or RIGHT OUTER JOIN): Retrieves all rows from the right table and matching rows from the left table.
FULL JOIN (or FULL OUTER JOIN): Retrieves all rows when there is a match in either the left or right table.
Subqueries:
Subqueries are queries nested within other queries. They can be used in SELECT, FROM, and WHERE clauses to retrieve or filter data based on the result of the subquery.
Aggregation:
Aggregation functions like COUNT, SUM, AVG, MIN, and MAX can be used to summarize data and calculate statistics.
GROUP BY and HAVING:
GROUP BY groups rows with identical values in specified columns and allows you to perform aggregation on each group.

HAVING is used to filter grouped data after the GROUP BY operation.
Window Functions:
Window functions, such as ROW_NUMBER, RANK, DENSE_RANK, and LAG, allow you to perform calculations across a set of table rows related to the current row.
UNION and UNION ALL:
UNION combines the result sets of two or more SELECT statements into a single result set, removing duplicates.
UNION ALL combines result sets but retains all rows, including duplicates.
Common Table Expressions (CTEs):
CTEs are temporary result sets that can be referenced within a SELECT, INSERT, UPDATE, or DELETE statement. They help break down complex queries into manageable parts.
Conditional Statements:
CASE statements allow conditional logic within SQL queries, enabling you to create calculated columns or modify query results based on conditions.
Stored Procedures and Functions:
Stored procedures and functions are reusable SQL code blocks that can be called with parameters to perform complex database operations.
Pivoting and Unpivoting:
Pivoting involves transforming rows into columns, while unpivoting does the reverse. These operations are often used in data reporting and analysis.
Substring and Pattern Matching:
SQL provides functions like SUBSTRING and regular expressions (e.g., REGEXP) for advanced text manipulation and pattern matching.
Handling Hierarchical Data:
Techniques like recursive common table expressions (CTEs) or the use of nested set models can be applied to work with hierarchical data structures.
Temporary Tables:
Temporary tables are tables that exist temporarily within a session, which can be useful for intermediate data storage during complex operations.
Optimization and Indexing:
Advanced querying often involves optimizing queries for performance, which may include creating and using indexes, and understanding execution plans.
These advanced SQL querying techniques are essential for working with complex data structures and performing in-depth data analysis. The specific techniques you need will depend on your use case and the complexity of the data you are working with.

3.6 MySQL Identifier Syntax and Naming Rules

MySQL has specific rules and syntax for naming identifiers, such as databases, tables, columns, indexes, and stored procedures. Adhering to these rules is essential to avoid errors and ensure that your SQL statements work correctly. Here are the key MySQL identifier naming rules and syntax:
Identifier Types:
MySQL supports the following types of identifiers:

- **Database Names:** Used to name databases.
- **Table Names:** Used to name tables within databases.
- **Column Names:** Used to name columns within tables.
- **Index Names:** Used to name indexes.
- **Stored Procedure Names:** Used to name stored procedures.
- **View Names:** Used to name views.

Character Set:
Identifiers can contain letters, numbers, and underscores.
MySQL supports various character sets for identifiers, such as Latin1, utf8, utf16, and more.
Length Limit:
The maximum length of an identifier depends on the storage engine and the character set used. For InnoDB with utf8, the limit is 767 bytes (767 characters).
Case Sensitivity:
By default, MySQL table and database names are case-insensitive on Windows and macOS but case-sensitive on Linux and other Unix-based systems.
You can control the case-sensitivity using system variables like **lower_case_table_names**.
Reserved Words:
Avoid using MySQL reserved words as identifiers. Reserved words are words that have a specific meaning in SQL and cannot be used as identifiers without quoting them. For example, "SELECT," "FROM," "JOIN" are reserved words.
Quoting Identifiers:
If you need to use a reserved word or an identifier that doesn't adhere to the naming rules, you can enclose it in backticks (`). For example:

```
CREATE TABLE `order` (id INT, order_date DATE);
```

Leading Digits:
Identifiers can start with a letter (a-z, A-Z), underscore (_), or dollar sign ($).
They cannot begin with a digit (0-9).
Special Characters:
Avoid using special characters, spaces, or non-alphanumeric characters in identifiers.
Stick to letters, numbers, and underscores for readability and compatibility.
Case Sensitivity of Collation:
When you use a case-insensitive collation for a column or table, comparisons and searches are case-insensitive.
You can specify collations at the column, table, or database level.
Local and System Variable Impact:
MySQL system variables like **lower_case_table_names** can affect identifier casing and case sensitivity. Be aware of the server's configuration.
It's good practice to choose meaningful and descriptive names for your identifiers, adhere to the rules and recommendations, and use consistent naming conventions to make your SQL code more readable and maintainable. Properly named identifiers also help avoid conflicts and errors when working with your database.

3.7 Case Sensitivity in SQL Statements

Case sensitivity in SQL statements refers to how the database management system treats the case (uppercase and lowercase) of letters in SQL keywords, identifiers (such as table and column names), and string comparisons. The handling of case sensitivity can vary between different database systems, including MySQL, PostgreSQL, SQL Server, and Oracle. Here's an overview of case sensitivity in SQL statements:
SQL Keywords:
SQL keywords, such as SELECT, FROM, WHERE, and JOIN, are typically not case-sensitive in most database systems. This means you can write these keywords in uppercase, lowercase, or any combination, and they will be treated the same. For example, all of the following are equivalent:
SELECT column1 FROM table1; select column1 from table1; Select column1 fRoM table1;
Identifiers (Table and Column Names):
The handling of case sensitivity for identifiers (e.g., table and column names) depends on the database system and configuration. Here are the common scenarios:
Case-Insensitive: In some database systems, such as SQL Server and Oracle, identifiers are case-insensitive by default. This means that "TableName" and "tablename" are treated as the same identifier.
Case-Preserving: Many database systems, including PostgreSQL, store identifiers as case-preserving but case-insensitive. This means that while the system stores the original casing of identifiers, it treats them as case-insensitive in SQL statements. For example, "TableName" and "tablename" are stored differently but treated as the same identifier in SQL statements.
Case-Sensitive: In MySQL, database systems running on Unix/Linux-based systems, and some configurations of SQL Server and Oracle, identifiers can be case-sensitive. In such systems, "TableName" and "tablename" would be treated as distinct identifiers.
String Comparisons:
In string comparisons (e.g., in the WHERE clause), the handling of case sensitivity is typically determined by the collation of the database, table, or column. Collation defines how characters are compared, including case sensitivity.
Case-Insensitive Collation: Using a case-insensitive collation means that string comparisons are case-insensitive. For example, "apple" and "Apple" are treated as the same string.
Case-Sensitive Collation: Using a case-sensitive collation means that string comparisons are case-sensitive. "apple" and "Apple" are treated as different strings.
Configuration and Collations:
Database systems often allow you to configure the case sensitivity behavior for identifiers and string comparisons. For example, you can specify collations at the column, table, or database level to control case sensitivity in string comparisons.
It's important to be aware of the case sensitivity behavior of the specific database system you are working with, as well as any collations and configurations that may affect it. Consistency in the use of case and careful consideration of collations are essential to avoid unexpected behavior in your SQL statements.

3.8 Creating, Dropping, Indexing, and Altering Tables

Creating, dropping, indexing, and altering tables are essential operations when working with a relational database like MySQL. These operations allow you to define the structure of your data, manage schema changes, and optimize query performance. Here's how to perform these tasks:
Creating Tables:
Creating tables involves defining the structure of your data, specifying column names, data types, constraints, and more. Here's an example of how to create a table in MySQL:

```
CREATE TABLE your_table_name (
   column1_name data_type constraints,
   column2_name data_type constraints,
   ...
);
```

Example:

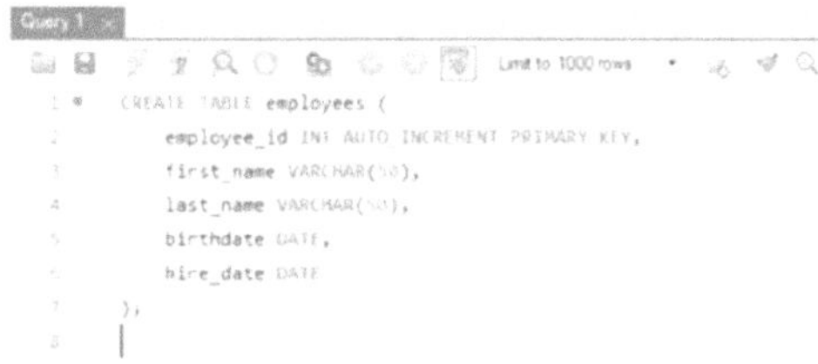

Dropping Tables:

Dropping a table removes it and all its data from the database. Be careful when using this operation, as it's irreversible.

DROP TABLE your_table_name;

Example:

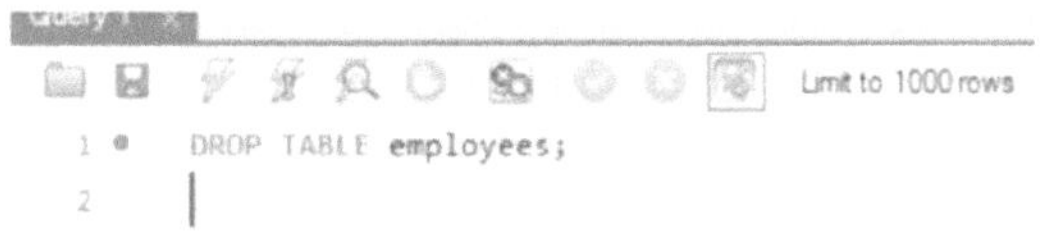

Indexing Tables:

Indexes are used to speed up data retrieval and query performance. You can create indexes on one or more columns to optimize common search operations. Here are some types of indexes in MySQL:

Single-Column Index:

CREATE INDEX index_name ON table_name (column_name);

Composite Index (Index on Multiple Columns):

CREATE INDEX index_name ON table_name (column1, column2);

Unique Index (No Duplicate Values):

CREATE UNIQUE INDEX index_name ON table_name (column_name);

Example:

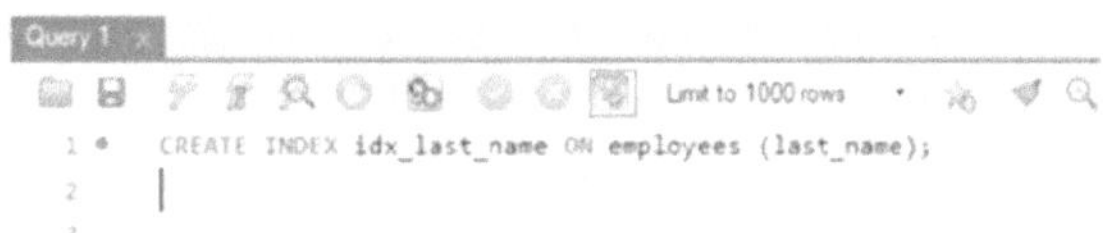

Altering Tables:

You may need to modify an existing table's structure over time. Use the **ALTER TABLE** statement for various alterations, including:

Adding a Column:

ALTER TABLE table_name
ADD column_name data_type constraints;

Modifying a Column (Changing Data Type or Constraints):

ALTER TABLE table_name
MODIFY column_name new_data_type new_constraints;

Renaming a Column:

ALTER TABLE table_name
CHANGE old_column_name new_column_name data_type constraints;

Dropping a Column:

ALTER TABLE table_name
DROP COLUMN column_name;

Adding or Dropping Constraints:

ALTER TABLE table_name
ADD CONSTRAINT constraint_name constraint_definition;

ALTER TABLE table_name
DROP CONSTRAINT constraint_name;

Example (adding a column):

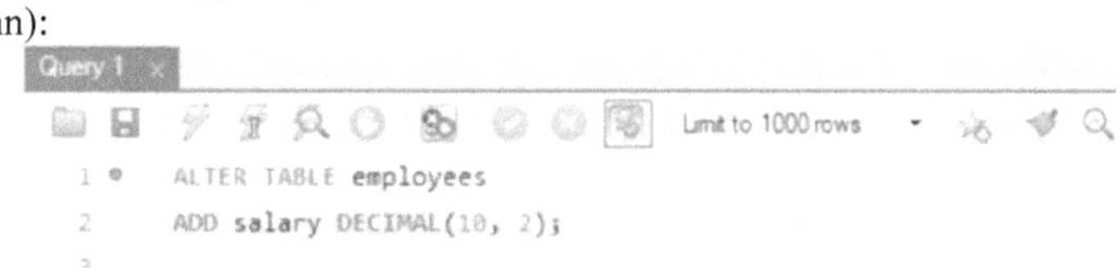

Renaming Tables:
To rename a table, use the **RENAME TABLE** statement:
RENAME TABLE old_table_name TO new_table_name;
Example:

Remember that altering tables can have a significant impact on your database and may require careful planning and testing, especially in a production environment. Be sure to back up your data before making structural changes, and consider the potential consequences on existing applications and queries.

3.9 Exercise

Exercise 1 – MCQ
Q 1. Which SQL statement is used to retrieve data from a database?
A) SELECT
B) INSERT
C) UPDATE
D) DELETE
Q 2. Which SQL clause is used to filter rows in a SELECT statement?
A) FROM
B) WHERE
C) ORDER BY
D) GROUP BY
Exercise 2 – True/ False
Q 1. In SQL, the SELECT statement is used for inserting new records into a table. (True/False)
Q 2. A JOIN operation in SQL combines rows from two or more tables into a single result set. (True/False)
Exercise 3 – Match case
Q 1. Match the following:
1) SELECT Statements
2) Filtering and Sorting Data
3) Joins and Subqueries
4) Inserting, Updating, and Deleting Data

a. Retrieves data from one or more tables.
b. Modifies existing records in a table.
c. Combines rows from two or more tables.
d. Narrows down rows based on specific conditions.
Exercise 4 – One word answer
Q 1. What does the SELECT statement do?
Q 2. What SQL clause is used to filter rows?
Exercise 5 – Small answer
Q 1. What SQL clause is used to filter rows based on specific conditions in a SELECT statement?
Q 2. In a SQL INSERT INTO statement, what does the VALUES clause specify?
Exercise 6 – Long answer
Q 1. Explain the use of the SELECT statement in SQL. Provide a detailed example of a complex SQL query that uses multiple clauses like WHERE, GROUP BY, HAVING, and ORDER BY. Describe each clause's purpose and how they contribute to the query's functionality. Additionally, discuss any potential performance considerations when using complex queries.
Q 2. Discuss the significance of joins and subqueries in SQL. Compare and contrast different types of joins, such as INNER JOIN, LEFT JOIN, and RIGHT JOIN, providing examples for each. Explain when it's appropriate to use subqueries instead of joins and vice versa, illustrating with practical scenarios. Highlight the advantages and limitations of each approach in terms of readability, performance, and maintainability in SQL queries.

Answer

Exercise 1
Answer 1: A), 2: B)
Exercise 2
Answer 1: False. 2: True.
Exercise 3
Answer 1: 1-a, 2-d, 3-c, 4-b.
Exercise 4

Answer 1: Retrieve, 2: WHERE

ONLINE RESOURCES

Practice Paper
Link: https://forms.gle/CQ1zCXmcib8yCWdz7
QR Code:

Video Content:
Link: https://www.youtube.com/playlist?list=PLzlh_31VWEFrZIhNdZoLo6Iuk6iy0PGEv
QR Code:

4.1 Data Modelling

Data 28odelling is a crucial process in database management that involves designing the structure of a database to ensure efficient data storage, retrieval, and manipulation. It serves as a blueprint for creating a database system that meets the needs of an organization or application. Let's explore data 28odelling in detail:

Key Concepts and Components:

Entity: An entity represents a real-world object or concept, such as a customer, product, or employee. Each entity has attributes that describe its properties.

Attribute: Attributes are characteristics or properties of entities. For example, a "Customer" entity may have attributes like "Name," "Address," and "Phone Number."

Relationship: Relationships define associations between entities. For instance, a "Customer" entity may have a relationship with an "Order" entity, indicating that customers can place orders.

Primary Key: A primary key is a unique identifier for each record in a database table. It ensures that each record is distinguishable and can be retrieved efficiently.

Foreign Key: A foreign key is a field in one table that establishes a link between that table and another table. It enforces referential integrity and defines relationships between tables.

Data Modeling Approaches:

Conceptual Data Model: This high-level model focuses on the overall structure of the database, including entities, their attributes, and the relationships between them. It doesn't concern itself with implementation details.

Logical Data Model: The logical data model translates the conceptual model into a more detailed representation, specifying data types, constraints, and relationships. It serves as the basis for database implementation.

Physical Data Model: The physical data model addresses the specific implementation aspects of the database, including table structures, indexing, and storage considerations. It is closely tied to the database management system being used.

Data Modeling Notations:

Entity-Relationship Diagram (ERD): ERDs visually represent entities, attributes, and relationships using symbols like rectangles (entities), ovals (attributes), and lines (relationships).

Unified Modeling Language (UML): UML provides a standardized way to model data structures, including class diagrams that resemble ERDs.

Normalization:

Normalization is a process that optimizes the database design by eliminating data redundancy and ensuring data integrity. It involves organizing data into tables and defining relationships between them to reduce anomalies like insertion, update, and deletion anomalies.

Denormalization:

Denormalization is the opposite of normalization, where redundancy is intentionally introduced to improve query performance. It's often used in situations where frequent complex queries are required, and the overhead of joins in normalized databases becomes a performance bottleneck.

Use of Data Modeling:

Database Design: Data 28odelling guides the creation of database schemas and structures, ensuring they align with the organization's requirements.

Data Integrity: Well-designed data models enforce data integrity constraints, preventing data inconsistencies and errors.

Performance Optimization: Effective data models can improve query performance and reduce database maintenance overhead.

Communication: Data models serve as a communication tool between stakeholders, including developers, database administrators, and business analysts.

Documentation: Data models document the structure and relationships within a database, aiding in understanding and maintenance.

Effective data 28odelling is fundamental to creating robust, efficient, and maintainable database systems. It lays the foundation for accurate data representation and retrieval, ensuring that organizations can leverage their data assets effectively for decision-making and business processes.

4.2 Entity-Relationship Diagrams (ERD)

Entity-Relationship Diagrams (ERDs) are graphical representations used in database design to visualize and model the structure of a database. ERDs provide a clear and concise way to depict entities, their attributes, and the relationships between them. Here's a detailed exploration of ERDs:

Key Components of ERD:

Entity: An entity represents a real-world object, concept, or thing with attributes that describe its properties. For example, "Customer" and "Product" are entities.

Attribute: Attributes are characteristics or properties of entities. They describe the details of an entity. For example, a "Customer" entity may have attributes like "Name," "Address," and "Email."

Relationship: Relationships define associations between entities. They indicate how entities are connected or interact with each other. For instance, a "Customer" entity may have a relationship with an "Order" entity, representing that customer place orders.

Types of Relationships:
One-to-One (1:1): One entity instance is associated with one instance of another entity. For example, one "Student" can have one "Student ID."
One-to-Many (1:N): One entity instance is associated with multiple instances of another entity. For example, one "Department" can have multiple "Employees."
Many-to-One (N:1): Multiple entity instances are associated with one instance of another entity. For example, multiple "Students" can belong to one "Class."
Many-to-Many (N:N): Multiple entity instances are associated with multiple instances of another entity. For example, "Students" enroll in multiple "Courses," and "Courses" have multiple "Students."
Components of ERD Diagrams:
Entities: Represented as rectangles with the entity name inside.
Attributes: Depicted as ovals connected to their respective entities by a line. Attributes are 29odellin with their names.
Relationships: Shown as lines connecting entities. Relationship lines may have diamonds at the ends to indicate cardinality (e.g., one or many).
Cardinality: Cardinality notations (1, N) indicate the number of instances on each side of a relationship.
Key Concepts in ERD Design:
Normalization: ERDs should guide the process of normalization, which involves organizing data to minimize data redundancy and improve data integrity.
Primary Keys: Each entity should have a primary key attribute that uniquely identifies each instance of that entity.
Foreign Keys: Relationships are often represented by foreign keys in related entities, ensuring referential integrity.
Use Cases and Benefits:
Database Design: ERDs are a fundamental tool for designing the structure of a database, helping define tables, attributes, and relationships.
Communication: ERDs facilitate communication between stakeholders, including developers, database administrators, and business analysts, by providing a visual representation of the database structure.
Documentation: ERDs serve as documentation for the database design, aiding in understanding and maintenance.
Query Planning: Database designers and developers use ERDs to plan and optimize queries, ensuring efficient data retrieval.
Data Integrity: ERDs help enforce data integrity constraints by defining relationships and cardinalities.
Scalability: ERDs provide insights into how entities and relationships may evolve with changing business needs.
ERDs are a foundational tool in database design and are instrumental in creating efficient and well-structured databases. They assist in visualizing complex data relationships and are essential for effective communication among database professionals and stakeholders during the design and development process.

4.3 Normalization Concepts

Normalization is a crucial database design process aimed at reducing data redundancy and ensuring data integrity by organizing data into well-structured tables. It involves breaking down larger tables into smaller, related tables while establishing relationships between them. The goal is to minimize data anomalies and improve database efficiency. Here's a detailed look at the concepts of normalization:
Key Concepts:
Functional Dependency: Functional dependency is a relationship between two attributes in a table, where one attribute's value determines the value of another attribute. It is denoted as A -> B, meaning attribute A determines attribute B.
Normalization Forms: There are several normalization forms, each with specific rules for organizing data. The most commonly used forms are:
First Normal Form (1NF): Ensures that each column in a table contains only atomic (indivisible) values, and there are no repeating groups or arrays.
Second Normal Form (2NF): Builds upon 1NF and eliminates partial dependencies by ensuring that non-key attributes depend on the entire primary key.
Third Normal Form (3NF): Builds upon 2NF and eliminates transitive dependencies by ensuring that non-key attributes depend only on the primary key, not on other non-key attributes.
Primary Key: A primary key is a unique identifier for each record in a table. It is essential for maintaining data integrity and ensuring that there are no duplicate rows in the table.
Candidate Key: Candidate keys are attributes or sets of attributes that can serve as a primary key for a table. They are unique and have no redundancy.
Benefits of Normalization:
Data Integrity: Normalization reduces data redundancy, which helps prevent data anomalies such as insertion, update, and deletion anomalies. This ensures data integrity.
Efficiency: Well-structured normalized tables make data retrieval and manipulation more efficient, as they require fewer joins and use disk space more optimally.
Scalability: Normalized databases are typically more scalable, as they can handle changes and additions to data without major restructuring.
Query Optimization: Normalization can lead to more straightforward and optimized queries, as it simplifies the structure of the database.
Normalization Process:

Identify Functional Dependencies: Determine which attributes depend on others within a table.
Remove Partial Dependencies (2NF): For tables not in 2NF, create separate tables for attributes that depend on only part of the primary key.
Remove Transitive Dependencies (3NF): For tables not in 3NF, create separate tables for attributes that depend on non-key attributes.
Create Relationships: Establish relationships between tables using foreign keys to maintain referential integrity.

Denormalization:

While normalization is generally a best practice, there are situations where denormalization may be appropriate. Denormalization intentionally introduces redundancy to improve query performance, especially in systems where read-heavy operations are common.

Use Cases:

OLAP (Online Analytical Processing): In data warehousing and business intelligence systems, denormalization can speed up complex analytical queries.
Caching: Denormalized data can be used for caching frequently accessed data for faster retrieval.
Normalization is a fundamental aspect of designing efficient and robust databases. It ensures data accuracy and consistency while facilitating efficient data retrieval and manipulation. However, the extent of normalization should be determined based on the specific needs and usage patterns of the database system.

4.4 Design Best Practices

Effective database design is critical for creating efficient, scalable, and maintainable database systems. Proper design ensures that data is stored, organized, and accessed optimally. Here are detailed best practices for designing databases:

Understand the Requirements:

Begin by thoroughly understanding the business requirements and data needs of the organization or application. Engage stakeholders to gather comprehensive requirements.

Normalize Data:

Normalize the database to reduce data redundancy and improve data integrity. Follow normalization rules (1NF, 2NF, 3NF) to organize data into well-structured tables.

Choose Appropriate Data Types:

Select the most suitable data types for each attribute to minimize storage requirements and ensure data accuracy. Use integer types for whole numbers, floating-point types for decimals, and character types for text.

Define Primary Keys:

Assign a unique primary key to each table to ensure data integrity. Typically, this is an auto-incrementing integer or a combination of attributes that uniquely identify each record.

Use Foreign Keys:

Establish relationships between tables using foreign keys to enforce referential integrity. This ensures that data consistency is maintained when records are linked between tables.

Index Strategically:

Create indexes on columns frequently used in WHERE clauses and JOIN conditions. However, avoid over-indexing, as it can lead to performance issues during data insertion and updates.

Plan for Scalability:

Design the database with scalability in mind. Consider how the database will handle increasing data volumes and user loads over time. Use partitioning and sharing techniques if necessary.

Implement Security Measures:

Enforce proper security measures, including authentication, authorization, and encryption, to protect sensitive data from unauthorized access.

Optimize Queries:

Write efficient SQL queries that leverage indexes and minimize unnecessary joins and subqueries. Use EXPLAIN or query plan tools to analyse query performance.

Consider Data Migration:

Plan for data migration processes, especially if you are transitioning from an existing database or integrating with other systems. Ensure data consistency during migration.

Backup and Recovery:

Implement robust backup and recovery procedures to safeguard data against unexpected events, such as hardware failures or data corruption.

Monitor Performance:

Continuously monitor database performance using monitoring tools and logs. Identify and address bottlenecks and performance issues promptly.

Documentation:

Maintain comprehensive documentation of the database schema, including table structures, relationships, and data dictionaries. This aids in understanding and maintenance.

Test Thoroughly:

Conduct thorough testing, including unit tests, integration tests, and performance tests, to ensure that the database functions as expected under various conditions.

Plan for Data Growth:

Anticipate data growth and plan for data archiving or purging strategies to manage historical data efficiently.

Consider Disaster Recovery:

Develop a disaster recovery plan to ensure data can be restored in case of catastrophic events like fires, floods, or data centre failures.

Keep Abreast of Technology:

Stay updated with advancements in database technology, including new features and best practices, to continually optimize your database systems.

Effective database design is an iterative process that requires ongoing refinement and adjustment as business requirements evolve. Following these best practices ensures that your database system is robust, efficient, and well-prepared to support the needs of the organization or application it serves.

4.5 The Entity Relationship Model

The Entity-Relationship (ER) model is a conceptual framework used in database design to represent the structure and relationships of data in a database. It is a graphical representation of entities (objects or concepts) and their relationships. The model uses several key components and subcomponents to describe the structure of data in a clear and concise manner. Let's delve into the Entity-Relationship model in detail with every key and subkey:

Entities:

Entities are the primary objects or concepts about which data is stored. Entities are represented by rectangles in an ER diagram. Each entity is described by:

Entity Name: The name of the entity, which is typically a noun.

Attributes:

Attributes represent the properties or characteristics of entities. Attributes are typically depicted within ovals and are connected to the respective entity by a line. Each attribute has:

Attribute Name: The name of the attribute, which is usually a noun.

Data Type: The type of data the attribute can store (e.g., string, integer, date).

Key Attribute: An attribute or a combination of attributes that uniquely identifies each instance of the entity.

Multivalued Attribute: An attribute that can hold multiple values for a single entity.

Derived Attribute: An attribute whose value can be derived from other attributes, typically through a calculation or formula.

Relationships:

Relationships define how entities are connected or related to each other. They are typically depicted as diamond shapes connecting the involved entities. Each relationship has:

Relationship Name: A verb or phrase describing the nature of the relationship between entities.

Degree: The number of participating entities in the relationship (e.g., binary, ternary).

Cardinality: Describes the number of instances of one entity that can be associated with the number of instances of the other entity in a relationship.

Role: Describes the role that each entity plays within the relationship.

Cardinality and Participation:

Cardinality and participation describe the nature of the relationship between entities more precisely. They are important subcomponents of relationships:

Cardinality:

One-to-One (1:1): Each entity in one set is related to only one entity in the other set.

One-to-Many (1:N): Each entity in one set can be related to multiple entities in the other set, but each entity in the other set can be related to only one entity in the first set.

Many-to-One (N:1): The reverse of one-to-many; multiple entities in one set can be related to one entity in the other set.

Many-to-Many (N:N): Multiple entities in one set can be related to multiple entities in the other set.

Participation:

Total Participation: Each entity in the set is involved in the relationship.

Partial Participation: Not every entity in the set is required to participate in the relationship.

Keys:

Keys are critical in entity-relationship modelling to ensure data integrity and uniqueness. There are different types of keys:

Primary Key (PK): An attribute (or set of attributes) that uniquely identifies each instance of an entity.

Composite Key: A primary key composed of multiple attributes.

Foreign Key (FK): An attribute (or set of attributes) in one entity that refers to the primary key of another entity, establishing a relationship between them.

Weak Entities:

A weak entity is an entity that cannot be uniquely identified by its attributes alone. It depends on a related entity (the strong entity) and has a partial key that is combined with the strong entity's key to form a unique identifier.

Subtypes and Supertypes:

Subtypes and supertypes represent hierarchical relationships between entities. Subtypes inherit attributes and relationships from their supertype.

Supertype: A generalized entity that has common attributes or relationships that are shared by its subtypes.

Subtype: A specialized entity that inherits attributes and relationships from a supertype and may have additional attributes and relationships.

The Entity-Relationship model is a powerful tool for designing databases by representing data entities, their attributes, relationships, and keys. Understanding the key components and subcomponents helps in creating clear and effective database schemas.

4.6 Entity Relationship Modelling Examples

Entity-Relationship Modelling (ER Modelling) is commonly used to design and represent the structure of a database. Here are some example scenarios and corresponding ER diagrams to help illustrate how ER modelling works:

Library Database:

Consider a library database where you want to keep track of books, authors, and borrowers. The ER diagram might look like this:

Entities:

Book
Author
Borrower

Attributes:

Book: ISBN, Title, Genre, Publication Year
Author: AuthorID, Name
Borrower: BorrowerID, Name, Contact Info

Relationships:

A book can have one or more authors (many-to-many relationship).
A borrower can borrow one or more books (many-to-many relationship).

MySQL Query for the above table:

```
-- Create Book table
CREATE TABLE Book (
    ISBN INT PRIMARY KEY,
    Title VARCHAR(255) NOT NULL,
    Genre VARCHAR(50),
    Publication_Year INT
);
-- Create Author table
CREATE TABLE Author (
    AuthorID INT PRIMARY KEY,
    Name VARCHAR(100) NOT NULL
);
-- Create Borrower table
CREATE TABLE Borrower (
    BorrowerID INT PRIMARY KEY,
    Name VARCHAR(100) NOT NULL,
    Contact_Info VARCHAR(255)
);
-- Create a junction table to represent the many-to-many relationship between Book and Author
CREATE TABLE Book_Author (
   Book_ISBN INT,
   Author_AuthorID INT,
   PRIMARY KEY (Book_ISBN, Author_AuthorID),
   FOREIGN KEY (Book_ISBN) REFERENCES Book(ISBN),
   FOREIGN KEY (Author_AuthorID) REFERENCES Author(AuthorID)
);
-- Create a junction table to represent the many-to-many relationship between Book and Borrower
CREATE TABLE Book_Borrower (
   Book_ISBN INT,
   Borrower_BorrowerID INT,
   Borrow_Date DATE,
   PRIMARY KEY (Book_ISBN, Borrower_BorrowerID),
   FOREIGN KEY (Book_ISBN) REFERENCES Book(ISBN),
   FOREIGN KEY (Borrower_BorrowerID) REFERENCES Borrower(BorrowerID)
);
```

E-commerce Store:

For an e-commerce store, you may need to track customers, products, orders, and payments. The ER diagram could look like this:

Entities:

Customer
Product
Order
Payment

Attributes:

Customer: CustomerID, Name, Email
Product: ProductID, Name, Price
Order: OrderID, Date, Status

Payment: PaymentID, Amount, Date

Relationships:

A customer can place many orders (one-to-many relationship).

An order can include one or more products (many-to-many relationship).

An order is associated with one payment (one-to-one relationship).

MySQL Query for the above table:

```sql
-- Create Customer table
CREATE TABLE Customer (
    CustomerID INT PRIMARY KEY,
    Name VARCHAR(100) NOT NULL,
    Email VARCHAR(255) UNIQUE
);
-- Create Product table
CREATE TABLE Product (
    ProductID INT PRIMARY KEY,
    Name VARCHAR(255) NOT NULL,
    Price DECIMAL(10, 2) NOT NULL
);
-- Create Order table
CREATE TABLE Order (
    OrderID INT PRIMARY KEY,
    Date DATE NOT NULL,
    Status VARCHAR(20) NOT NULL,
    CustomerID INT,
    FOREIGN KEY (CustomerID) REFERENCES Customer(CustomerID)
);
-- Create Order_Product junction table to represent the many-to-many relationship between Order and Product
CREATE TABLE Order_Product (
    OrderID INT,
    ProductID INT,
    Quantity INT,
    PRIMARY KEY (OrderID, ProductID),
    FOREIGN KEY (OrderID) REFERENCES Order(OrderID),
    FOREIGN KEY (ProductID) REFERENCES Product(ProductID)
);
-- Create Payment table
CREATE TABLE Payment (
    PaymentID INT PRIMARY KEY,
    Amount DECIMAL(10, 2) NOT NULL,
    Date DATE NOT NULL,
    OrderID INT,
    FOREIGN KEY (OrderID) REFERENCES Order(OrderID)
);
```

University Database:

For a university database, you'll want to keep track of students, courses, professors, and enrollments. The ER diagram might look like this:

Entities:

Student

Course

Professor

Enrollment

Attributes:

Student: StudentID, Name, Email

Course: CourseID, Title, Credits

Professor: ProfessorID, Name, Department

Enrollment: EnrollmentID, Date

Relationships:

A student can enroll in many courses (many-to-many relationship).

A course can have many students (many-to-many relationship).

A professor can teach many courses (one-to-many relationship).

An enrollment is associated with one student, one course, and one professor (one-to-one relationships).

MySQL Query for the above table:

```sql
-- Create Student table
CREATE TABLE Student (
    StudentID INT PRIMARY KEY,
    Name VARCHAR(100) NOT NULL,
    Email VARCHAR(255) UNIQUE
);
-- Create Course table
CREATE TABLE Course (
    CourseID INT PRIMARY KEY,
    Title VARCHAR(255) NOT NULL,
    Credits INT NOT NULL
);
-- Create Professor table
CREATE TABLE Professor (
    ProfessorID INT PRIMARY KEY,
    Name VARCHAR(100) NOT NULL,
    Department VARCHAR(50)
);
-- Create Enrollment table
CREATE TABLE Enrollment (
    EnrollmentID INT PRIMARY KEY,
    Date DATE NOT NULL,
    StudentID INT,
    CourseID INT,
    ProfessorID INT,
    FOREIGN KEY (StudentID) REFERENCES Student(StudentID),
    FOREIGN KEY (CourseID) REFERENCES Course(CourseID),
    FOREIGN KEY (ProfessorID) REFERENCES Professor(ProfessorID)
);
```

These are simplified examples to illustrate the concept of ER 34odelling. In real-world scenarios, databases can become more complex with additional entities, attributes, and relationships. ER 34odelling provides a visual representation of how data is structured and related, making it an essential step in database design.

4.7 Table Retrievals with Joins

able retrievals with joins involve using SQL statements to retrieve data from multiple tables by combining rows based on specified relationships. Joins are essential for querying databases with related information distributed across different tables. There are different types of joins in SQL, including INNER JOIN, LEFT JOIN, RIGHT JOIN, and FULL JOIN, and each serves a specific purpose.

Here's a basic overview of these join types and how to retrieve data from related tables:

INNER JOIN:

An INNER JOIN returns only the rows that have matching values in both tables. It combines rows from two tables where the specified condition is met.

```sql
SELECT column1, column2
FROM table1
INNER JOIN table2
ON table1.column = table2.column;
```

LEFT JOIN (or LEFT OUTER JOIN):

A LEFT JOIN returns all the rows from the left table and the matching rows from the right table. If there is no match, NULL values are returned for columns from the right table.

```sql
SELECT column1, column2
FROM table1
LEFT JOIN table2
ON table1.column = table2.column;
```

RIGHT JOIN (or RIGHT OUTER JOIN):

A RIGHT JOIN is similar to a LEFT JOIN, but it returns all the rows from the right table and the matching rows from the left table. If there is no match, NULL values are returned for columns from the left table.

```sql
SELECT column1, column2
FROM table1
RIGHT JOIN table2
ON table1.column = table2.column;
```

FULL JOIN (or FULL OUTER JOIN):

A FULL JOIN returns all rows from both tables, including the rows where there is no match. If there is no match, NULL values are returned for columns from the table without a match.

```sql
SELECT column1, column2
FROM table1
FULL JOIN table2
ON table1.column = table2.column;
```

Example:

Let's say we have a **Students** table and a **Courses** table, and we want to retrieve a list of students along with the courses they are enrolled in using INNER JOIN:

```sql
SELECT Students.StudentName, Courses.CourseName
FROM Students
INNER JOIN Enrollments
ON Students.StudentID = Enrollments.StudentID
INNER JOIN Courses
ON Enrollments.CourseID = Courses.CourseID;
```

In this example, we're retrieving the names of students and the names of the courses they are enrolled in by joining the **Students**, **Enrollments**, and **Courses** tables using INNER JOIN.

You can adapt these SQL statements to your specific database and table structure to retrieve data from related tables using different types of joins, depending on your needs.

4.8 Exercise

Exercise 1 – MCQ

Q 1. Which SQL statement is used to insert new data into a database?
A) SELECT
B) UPDATE
C) INSERT
D) DELETE

Q 2. What is the primary goal of database design best practices?
A) Maximize data redundancy
B) Minimize data integrity
C) Optimize database performance
D) Avoid normalization

Exercise 2 – True/ False

Q 1. When you want to delete a record from a database table, it's a best practice to directly remove it from the table without considering any dependencies.

Q 2. Creating numerous indexes on all columns of a table is not a recommended practice. While indexes can improve query performance, excessive indexing can lead to overhead during data insertion and updates. Indexes should be added strategically to columns that are frequently used in WHERE clauses and JOIN conditions.

Exercise 3 – One word answer

Q 1. What notation in an ERD indicates the number of instances related in a relationship?

Q 2. What is a unique identifier for each record in a table, ensuring data integrity?

Exercise 4 – Small answer

Q 1. What is the purpose of the INSERT statement in SQL?

Q 2. How does the DELETE statement work in SQL?

Exercise 5 – Long answer

Q 1. Inserting, updating, and deleting data are fundamental operations in a database system. Explain the significance of these operations and discuss some common challenges associated with them.

Q 2. Discuss the role of Entity-Relationship Diagrams (ERD) in the database design process. Explain how ERDs help in visualizing and planning database structures, and provide an example of an ERD for a specific scenario.

Answer

Exercise 1

Answer 1: C) INSERT, 2: C) Optimize database performance

Exercise 2

Answer 1: False, 2: False.

Exercise 3

Answer 1: Cardinality, 2: Primary Key.

ONLINE RESOURCES

Practice Paper
Link: https://forms.gle/dsoQsYkz5sSBUkvN7
QR Code:

Video Content:
Link: https://www.youtube.com/playlist?list=PLzlh_31VWEFp6Rk5MmSOYtphClAq7D05J
QR Code:

Chapter 5: Design Best Practices

5.1 Creating and Modifying Tables

Creating and modifying tables are fundamental operations in database management. You use SQL commands to define the structure of your tables and make changes as needed. Here's how to create and modify tables in a relational database using SQL:

Creating Tables:

To create a new table, you use the **CREATE TABLE** statement. Here's the basic syntax:

```
CREATE TABLE table_name (
    column1 datatype constraints,
    column2 datatype constraints,
    ...
);
```

table_name: The name of the table you want to create.
column1, **column2**, ...: The names of the columns in the table.
datatype: The data type of each column, such as INT, VARCHAR, DATE, etc.
constraints: Optional constraints like PRIMARY KEY, UNIQUE, NOT NULL, and others to define column behavior.

Here's an example of creating a "Students" table:

```
CREATE TABLE Students (
    StudentID INT PRIMARY KEY,
    FirstName VARCHAR(50),
    LastName VARCHAR(50),
    Birthdate DATE,
    Email VARCHAR(100) UNIQUE
);
```

This SQL statement creates a table named "Students" with columns for student information.

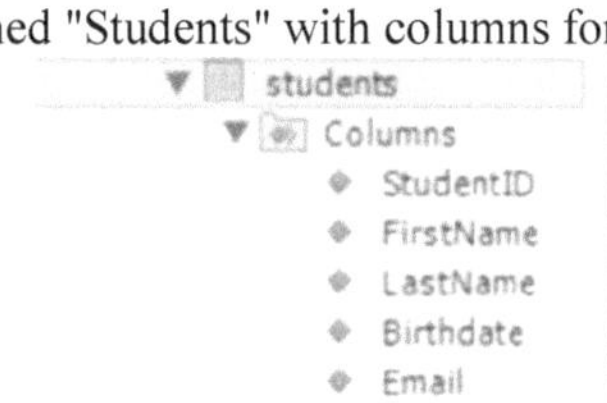

Modifying Tables:

To modify an existing table, you use the **ALTER TABLE** statement. You can add, modify, or remove columns and constraints. Here are some common operations:

Adding a Column:

ALTER TABLE table_name
ADD column_name datatype constraints;

Modifying a Column (Changing Data Type or Constraints):

ALTER TABLE table_name
MODIFY column_name new_datatype new_constraints;

Renaming a Column:

ALTER TABLE table_name
CHANGE old_column_name new_column_name new_datatype new_constraints;

Dropping a Column:

ALTER TABLE table_name
DROP COLUMN column_name;

Adding or Dropping Constraints:

ALTER TABLE table_name
ADD CONSTRAINT constraint_name constraint_definition;

ALTER TABLE table_name
DROP CONSTRAINT constraint_name;

Here are examples of modifying a table:

Adding a new column "PhoneNumber" to the "Students" table:

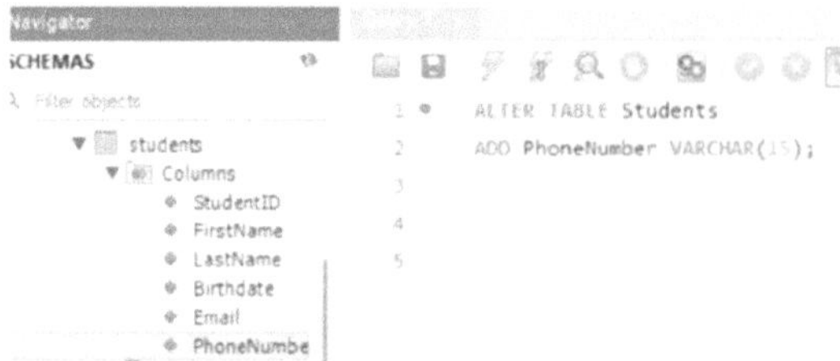

Modifying the data type and adding a constraint to the "Email" column:

Renaming the "FirstName" column to "First_Name" and changing its data type:

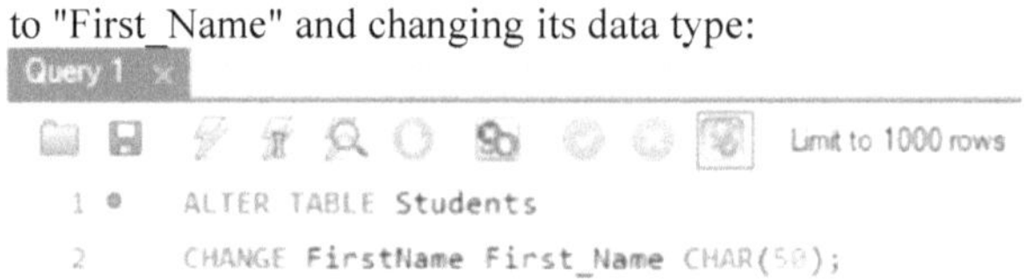

Dropping the "Birthdate" column from the "Students" table:

Adding a UNIQUE constraint to the "StudentID" column:

Dropping the UNIQUE constraint on the "Email" column:

Make sure to carefully plan and execute table modifications, especially in a production environment, as these changes can impact your data and applications. Always back up your data and consider the potential consequences of the modifications.

5.2 Creating and Using Views

Views in a relational database are virtual tables that represent the result of a SELECT query. They allow you to simplify complex queries, provide an additional layer of security, and present a tailored perspective of your data to users. Here's how to create and use views in SQL:

Creating Views:

To create a view, you use the **CREATE VIEW** statement. The basic syntax is as follows:

```
CREATE VIEW view_name AS
SELECT column1, column2, ...
FROM table_name
WHERE condition;
```

view_name: The name you give to the view.
column1, column2, ...: The columns you want to include in the view.
table_name: The name of the table you are querying.
condition: An optional condition to filter the data in the view.

Example:

Suppose you have a "Students" table, and you want to create a view that displays only the students who have a GPA above 3.0:

```
CREATE VIEW HighGPAStudents AS
SELECT StudentID, FirstName, LastName, GPA
FROM Students
WHERE GPA > 3.0;
```

This creates a view called "HighGPAStudents" that displays the selected columns from the "Students" table for students with a GPA above 3.0.

Using Views:

Once you've created a view, you can use it just like a regular table in your SQL queries. For example, you can perform SELECT, INSERT, UPDATE, and DELETE operations on views. Here are some examples:

SELECT from a View:

You can query a view to retrieve data just as you would from a table:

```
SELECT * FROM HighGPAStudents;
```

INSERT into a View:

You can insert data into a view if it's updatable, meaning it's based on a single table without aggregation or joins. The data will be inserted into the underlying table.

```
INSERT INTO HighGPAStudents (StudentID, FirstName, LastName, GPA)
VALUES (101, 'John', 'Doe', 3.5);
```

UPDATE a View:

If a view is updatable, you can update the data within it. Changes will be applied to the underlying table.

```
UPDATE HighGPAStudents
SET GPA = 3.7
WHERE StudentID = 102;
```

DELETE from a View:

Deleting from a view will delete data from the underlying table.

```
DELETE FROM HighGPAStudents
WHERE StudentID = 103;
```

Modifying Views:

To modify the definition of a view, you can use the **ALTER VIEW** statement to change the query that defines the view.

```
ALTER VIEW view_name AS
SELECT new_columns
FROM new_table
WHERE new_condition;
```

Dropping Views:

To remove a view, you use the **DROP VIEW** statement:

```
DROP VIEW view_name;
```

Views can be a powerful tool for simplifying complex queries, enhancing security by limiting access to sensitive data, and providing a more user-friendly interface to your database. However, they come with some performance considerations, so it's essential to use them judiciously and understand their impact on your database.

5.3 Temporary Tables and Table Variables

Temporary tables and table variables are used in SQL to store and manipulate data temporarily within the scope of a single session or query. They are particularly useful for storing intermediate results, reducing the complexity of queries, and managing data during complex operations. Let's explore temporary tables and table variables in detail, along with examples.

Temporary Tables:

Temporary tables are created and used for the duration of a database session or until they are explicitly dropped. They are typically used to hold intermediate results or to simplify complex queries.

Creating Temporary Tables:

In SQL, you can create temporary tables by prefixing the table name with a single hash (#) for temporary tables in SQL Server or by using the "TEMP" keyword for temporary tables in MySQL and PostgreSQL.

Example (SQL Server):

```
-- Create a temporary table in SQL Server
CREATE TABLE #TempOrders (
   OrderID INT,
   CustomerName VARCHAR(50),
   OrderDate DATE
);
```

Example (MySQL and PostgreSQL):

Inserting Data into Temporary Tables:

You can insert data into temporary tables just like regular tables.

```
-- Insert data into the temporary table
INSERT INTO #TempOrders (OrderID, CustomerName, OrderDate)
VALUES (1, 'John Doe', '2023-01-15');
```

Selecting Data from Temporary Tables:

You can query data from temporary tables as you would from regular tables.

```
-- Select data from the temporary table
SELECT * FROM #TempOrders;
```

Dropping Temporary Tables:

Temporary tables are automatically dropped when the session ends, but you can also explicitly drop them.

```
-- Explicitly drop the temporary table
DROP TABLE #TempOrders;
```

Table Variables:

Table variables are another way to store temporary data, and they are primarily used in SQL Server. Unlike temporary tables, table variables are declared using a DECLARE statement and do not require explicit dropping.

Declaring and Using Table Variables:

```
-- Declare a table variable
DECLARE @TableVariable TABLE (
   Column1 INT,
   Column2 VARCHAR(50)
);

-- Insert data into the table variable
INSERT INTO @TableVariable (Column1, Column2)
VALUES (1, 'Value1'), (2, 'Value2');

-- Select data from the table variable
SELECT * FROM @TableVariable;
```

Table variables are a good choice when you need to store temporary data within a query or procedure, and you don't want to explicitly drop them. They have certain limitations, such as not supporting indexes or being less efficient for very large data sets, so you should choose the appropriate method based on your specific use case.

Remember that the syntax for creating and using temporary tables or table variables can vary slightly depending on the database management system you are using, so consult your DBMS documentation for exact details.

5.4 Exercise

Q1. Which SQL statement is used to create a new table in a database?
a. CREATE TABLE
b. ADD TABLE
c. INSERT INTO
d. MODIFY TABLE
Q2. What is the purpose of the PRIMARY KEY constraint in a table?
a. It ensures that each column has a unique value.
b. It allows null values in a column.
c. It enforces referential integrity.
d. It specifies the data type of a column.
Q3. In SQL, which data type is typically used for storing textual data of varying length?
a. INT
b. CHAR
c. VARCHAR
d. DATE
Q4. Which SQL command is used to add a new column to an existing table?
a. ALTER TABLE
b. CREATE TABLE
c. UPDATE TABLE
d. MODIFY TABLE
Q5. What SQL statement is used to remove a table from a database?
a. DELETE TABLE
b. DROP TABLE
c. REMOVE TABLE
d. ERASE TABLE
Q6. Which keyword is used to specify that a column cannot contain NULL values?
a. NOT NULL
b. UNIQUE
c. PRIMARY KEY
d. AUTO_INCREMENT
Q7. What SQL command is used to change the name of an existing table?
a. RENAME TABLE
b. CHANGE TABLE
c. MODIFY TABLE
d. ALTER TABLE
Q8. In a relational database, which statement is true about the FOREIGN KEY constraint?
a. It enforces uniqueness in a column.
b. It ensures that a column contains only numeric values.
c. It establishes a link between two tables based on a column.
d. It allows duplicate values in a column.
Q9. What is the purpose of the AUTO_INCREMENT attribute in MySQL?
a. It automatically assigns a unique value to the primary key column.
b. It specifies the maximum value a column can hold.
c. It adds a new row to the table.
d. It orders the table rows alphabetically.
Q10. Which SQL command is used to modify an existing table, including changing column data types?
a. ALTER TABLE
b. UPDATE TABLE
c. MODIFY TABLE
d. CHANGE TABLE
Q11. In MySQL, what is the purpose of the UNIQUE constraint on a column?
a. It enforces that the column contains only unique values.
b. It allows NULL values in the column.
c. It sets the default value for the column.
d. It specifies the data type of the column.
Q12. Which SQL statement is used to add a default value to an existing column?
a. ALTER TABLE
b. MODIFY TABLE
c. DEFAULT VALUE

d. ADD COLUMN
Q13. What is the purpose of the CHECK constraint in a table?
a. It enforces referential integrity between tables.
b. It checks for valid values in a column based on a specified condition.
c. It ensures that a column contains only NULL values.
d. It adds a new column to the table.
Q14. Which SQL statement is used to rename a column in an existing table?
a. RENAME COLUMN
b. CHANGE COLUMN
c. MODIFY COLUMN
d. ALTER COLUMN
Q15. What is the purpose of the INDEX keyword in the context of creating tables?
a. It creates a new table.
b. It defines a primary key column.
c. It creates an index on a table column for faster data retrieval.
d. It specifies the character set of the table.
Q16. What is a temporary table in a database?
a. A table that is permanently stored in the database
b. A table used to store temporary data that exists only for the duration of a database session
c. A table that is replicated across multiple database servers
d. A table used for storing historical data
Q17. Which of the following databases supports temporary tables?
a. MySQL
b. NoSQL databases
c. MongoDB
d. PostgreSQL
Q18. In MySQL, how is a temporary table's data typically preserved?
a. Data is permanently stored in the table until manually deleted
b. Data is stored for the duration of the session and is automatically dropped when the session ends
c. Data is stored until the server is restarted
d. Data is stored until the database schema is modified
Q19. What is the scope of a temporary table in SQL Server?
a. Limited to the current transaction
b. Limited to the current query
c. Limited to the current session
d. Global across all sessions
Q20. Which SQL command is used to create a temporary table in SQL Server?
a. CREATE TABLE
b. CREATE TEMPORARY TABLE
c. CREATE GLOBAL TEMPORARY TABLE
d. DECLARE @table TABLE
Q21. What is the advantage of using table variables over temporary tables in SQL Server?
a. Table variables are permanent and can store data indefinitely.
b. Table variables are faster for storing large datasets.
c. Table variables are stored in memory and are typically faster for smaller datasets.
d. There is no advantage; they are functionally identical.
Q22. In PostgreSQL, how are temporary tables created?
a. Using the CREATE TABLE statement with the TEMP keyword
b. Using the DECLARE statement
c. Using the CREATE TEMPORARY TABLE statement
d. Temporary tables are not supported in PostgreSQL.
Q23. Which of the following is true about temporary tables in databases?
a. Temporary tables can be indexed.
b. Temporary tables can be used to store data permanently.
c. Temporary tables can be accessed by multiple sessions simultaneously.
d. Temporary tables can only be created by database administrators.
Q24. In SQL Server, what is the naming convention for table variables?
a. Prefix with @
b. Prefix with #

c. Prefix with $
d. No specific naming convention
Q25. What happens to a temporary table in SQL Server when the session that created it ends?
a. The table is permanently deleted.
b. The table is automatically dropped.
c. The table remains, and data is retained.
d. The table's scope extends to all sessions.
Q26. In MySQL, which storage engine is commonly used for temporary tables?
a. InnoDB
b. MyISAM
c. MEMORY
d. NDB
Q27. Which of the following database systems does not support temporary tables or table variables?
a. Oracle Database
b. SQLite
c. MySQL
d. SQL Server
Q28. What is the primary use case for table variables in SQL Server?
a. Storing data for long-term historical analysis
b. Storing intermediate results during complex queries
c. Storing data shared across multiple sessions
d. Storing large datasets for reporting
Q29. In PostgreSQL, what keyword is used to create a temporary table that is accessible by all sessions?
a. GLOBAL
b. SHARED
c. TEMP
d. PUBLIC
Q30. Which SQL statement is used to drop a temporary table in MySQL?
a. DROP DATABASE
b. DROP TABLE
c. DELETE TABLE
d. DELETE DATABASE

Answer

1) a. 2) a. 3) c. 4) a. 5) b. 6) a. 7) a. 8) c. 9) a. 10) a. 11) a. 12) a. 13) b. 14) b. 15) c. 16) b. 17) a. 18) b. 19) c. 20) c. 21) c. 22) a. 23) a. 24) a. 25) b. 26) c. 27) a. 28) b. 29) c. 30) b.

ONLINE RESOURCES

Practice Paper
Link: https://forms.gle/nXo5JaFdFdXVXBrn8
QR Code:

Video Content:
Link: https://www.youtube.com/playlist?list=PLzlh_31VWEFp7iVY0eeEGf-Kj6hG2U2wh
QR Code:

Chapter 6: Stored Procedures and Functions

6.1 Creating and Managing Stored Procedures

Stored procedures in MySQL are precompiled, reusable SQL code that can be executed with a single call. They are used for encapsulating business logic, improving performance, and providing security in database operations. Here's a detailed guide on creating and managing stored procedures in MySQL:

Creating a Stored Procedure:

To create a stored procedure in MySQL, use the **CREATE PROCEDURE** statement. The basic syntax is as follows:

```
DELIMITER //
CREATE PROCEDURE procedure_name ([parameter1 datatype], [parameter2 datatype], ...)
BEGIN
    -- SQL statements for the procedure
END //
DELIMITER ;
```

DELIMITER //: Changes the statement delimiter temporarily so that semicolons within the procedure body are treated as part of the statement.

procedure_name: The name of the stored procedure.

parameter1, parameter2, ...: Parameters that can be passed to the procedure. They are optional.

BEGIN and **END**: Enclose the body of the procedure, where you write your SQL statements.

Example:

Let's create a simple stored procedure that retrieves the total number of students in a given department:

```
DELIMITER //
CREATE PROCEDURE GetStudentCountByDepartment(IN departmentName VARCHAR(50))
BEGIN
    SELECT COUNT(*) FROM Students WHERE Department = departmentName;
END //
DELIMITER ;
```

Calling a Stored Procedure:

To call a stored procedure, you can use the **CALL** statement:

```
CALL GetStudentCountByDepartment('Computer Science');
```

Altering a Stored Procedure:

To modify an existing stored procedure, you can use the **ALTER PROCEDURE** statement:

```
ALTER PROCEDURE procedure_name ([parameter1 datatype], [parameter2 datatype], ...)
BEGIN
    -- Updated SQL statements for the procedure
END;
```

Example:

```
DELIMITER //
ALTER PROCEDURE GetStudentCountByDepartment(IN departmentName VARCHAR(50))
BEGIN
    SELECT COUNT(*) FROM Students WHERE DepartmentName = departmentName;
END //
DELIMITER ;
```

Dropping a Stored Procedure:

To remove a stored procedure, use the DROP PROCEDURE statement:

DROP PROCEDURE procedure_name;

Managing Parameters:

Stored procedures can have input (IN), output (OUT), or input/output (INOUT) parameters. Parameters are used to pass values into and out of the procedure. Here's how to declare and use parameters:

```
CREATE PROCEDURE CalculateSum(IN a INT, IN b INT, OUT result INT)
BEGIN
    SET result = a + b;
END;
```

You can then call this procedure and retrieve the result:

```
CALL CalculateSum(5, 7, @sum);
SELECT @sum;
```

Flow Control in Stored Procedures:

You can use conditional statements (IF, CASE), loops (WHILE, REPEAT, LOOP), and cursors in stored procedures to control the flow of execution and perform complex logic.

Example with IF:

```
CREATE PROCEDURE CheckGPA(IN studentID INT)
BEGIN
  DECLARE gpa DECIMAL(3, 2);
  SELECT GPA INTO gpa FROM Students WHERE StudentID = studentID;

  IF gpa >= 3.0 THEN
    SELECT 'Good standing';
  ELSE
    SELECT 'Academic probation';
  END IF;
END;
```

Example with CURSOR:

```
CREATE PROCEDURE GetAllStudents()
BEGIN
  DECLARE done INT DEFAULT 0;
  DECLARE studentName VARCHAR(100);
  DECLARE cur CURSOR FOR SELECT StudentName FROM Students;
  DECLARE CONTINUE HANDLER FOR NOT FOUND SET done = 1;

  OPEN cur;
  read_loop: LOOP
    FETCH cur INTO studentName;
    IF done THEN
      LEAVE read_loop;
    END IF;
    -- Process studentName
  END LOOP;
  CLOSE cur;
END;
```

Stored procedures in MySQL offer a powerful way to encapsulate database logic, enhance security, and improve performance. You can create and manage them based on your specific application needs.

6.2 User-Defined Functions (UDFs)

User-Defined Functions (UDFs) in the context of a database are custom functions created by users or developers to extend the functionality of a database management system (DBMS). UDFs allow you to encapsulate custom business logic, calculations, or data processing within the database, making it easier to reuse and maintain code. They are supported in various database systems, including MySQL, PostgreSQL, SQL Server, and others.

Here's a general overview of User-Defined Functions and how they work:

Types of UDFs:

Scalar Functions: These functions take one or more input values and return a single output value. Scalar functions are often used for calculations and data transformation. For example, you can create a scalar UDF to calculate the age of a person based on their birthdate.

Table-Valued Functions: These functions return a result set in the form of a table. Table-valued functions are useful for complex queries that need to return multiple rows and columns. They can be used in SELECT statements just like regular tables.

Aggregate Functions: Aggregate UDFs operate on a set of values and return a single result, such as SUM, AVG, COUNT, MAX, or MIN. You can create custom aggregate functions to perform specialized calculations.

Creating UDFs:

The process of creating UDFs varies depending on the database management system you're using. Here's a simplified example of creating a scalar UDF in MySQL:

```
DELIMITER //
CREATE FUNCTION CalculateAge(birthdate DATE)
RETURNS INT
BEGIN
    DECLARE today DATE;
    DECLARE age INT;

    SET today = CURDATE();
    SET age = YEAR(today) - YEAR(birthdate);

    IF DATE_FORMAT(today, '%m%d') < DATE_FORMAT(birthdate, '%m%d') THEN
        SET age = age - 1;
    END IF;

    RETURN age;
END //
DELIMITER ;
```

This example defines a scalar UDF named "CalculateAge" that takes a birthdate as input and returns the age.

Using UDFs:

Once you've created a UDF, you can use it in your SQL queries just like built-in functions. For example:

SELECT FirstName, LastName, CalculateAge(BirthDate) AS Age FROM Customers;

In this query, the "CalculateAge" UDF is used to calculate the age of customers based on their birthdate.

Advantages of UDFs:

Code Reusability: UDFs allow you to reuse custom logic across multiple queries and applications.

Encapsulation: UDFs encapsulate logic within the database, promoting clean code and separation of concerns.

Performance: UDFs can improve query performance by executing logic on the database server rather than transferring data to be processed on the client side.

Considerations:

UDFs can be resource-intensive. Complex UDFs may impact database performance, so it's essential to optimize their code.

UDFs are specific to the database system you're using, and their syntax can vary between systems.

User-Defined Functions are a powerful tool for extending the functionality of a database and enabling developers to work with data in a more customized and efficient way.

6.3 Error Handling and Transactions

Error handling and transactions are critical aspects of database management and development. They ensure data integrity, consistency, and reliability in database operations. Let's explore these concepts in detail:

Error Handling:

Error handling in the context of a database involves dealing with unexpected issues that can arise during SQL statements' execution. These issues can include constraint violations, data type mismatches, missing data, and other runtime errors. Proper error handling is essential to prevent data corruption and maintain the stability of the database.

In SQL, error handling is typically done using constructs like TRY...CATCH (SQL Server), BEGIN...EXCEPTION (PL/SQL in Oracle), or DECLARE...HANDLER (MySQL).

Example (MySQL):

```
BEGIN
  -- Attempt to insert data
  INSERT INTO Students (StudentID, FirstName, LastName)
  VALUES (1, 'John', 'Doe');

  -- Handle any exceptions
  DECLARE CONTINUE HANDLER FOR SQLEXCEPTION
  BEGIN
    ROLLBACK; -- Rollback the transaction
    SELECT 'An error occurred' AS Error;
  END;

  -- Commit the transaction if there are no errors
  COMMIT;
END;
```

In this MySQL example, a transaction is used to insert data into the "Students" table. If an exception occurs, it's caught, and the transaction is rolled back. Otherwise, it's committed.

Transactions:

A transaction is a sequence of one or more SQL statements that are treated as a single unit of work. Transactions are essential to maintain data consistency and integrity in a database, especially in a multi-user environment. The four fundamental properties of transactions are often referred to as ACID:

Atomicity: A transaction is treated as a single, indivisible unit of work. It either completes all its operations or none at all. If any part of a transaction fails, the entire transaction is rolled back.

Consistency: A transaction brings the database from one consistent state to another consistent state. It ensures that data remains valid and follows any defined constraints.
Isolation: Transactions are executed as if they are the only operations occurring in the database. This prevents data corruption due to concurrent access.
Durability: Once a transaction is committed, its effects are permanent and will survive any subsequent system failures.
Example (SQL Server):

```
BEGIN TRANSACTION;

-- Insert data into multiple tables
INSERT INTO Orders (OrderID, CustomerID, OrderDate) VALUES (1, 101, '2023-10-01');
INSERT INTO OrderDetails (OrderID, ProductID, Quantity) VALUES (1, 201, 3);

-- If everything is successful, commit the transaction
COMMIT TRANSACTION;

-- If an error occurs or you want to cancel the transaction, use ROLLBACK instead of COMMIT
```

In this SQL Server example, a transaction is initiated using **BEGIN TRANSACTION**, and a series of SQL statements is executed. If everything is successful, the transaction is committed using **COMMIT TRANSACTION**. If an error occurs or you want to cancel the transaction, you can use **ROLLBACK** instead of **COMMIT**.
Proper error handling and transaction management are crucial for maintaining data integrity and reliability in database operations, especially in production environments where concurrent access and unforeseen errors can occur. These techniques help ensure that data remains accurate and consistent even in the face of unexpected events.

6.4 Dynamic SQL and Cursors

Dynamic SQL and cursors are two important features in database programming. They are often used to handle dynamic, flexible queries and to iterate through result sets. Let's explore these concepts in more detail:
Dynamic SQL:
Dynamic SQL refers to the practice of creating and executing SQL statements at runtime, allowing for flexibility in query construction. Dynamic SQL is useful when you need to build SQL statements based on user input, application logic, or other dynamic factors.
In dynamic SQL, you typically construct SQL statements as strings and then execute those strings as SQL commands. Here's an example in SQL Server:

```
DECLARE @sql NVARCHAR(MAX);
DECLARE @param INT = 123;

SET @sql = 'SELECT * FROM YourTable WHERE ID = ' + CAST(@param AS NVARCHAR(10));
EXEC sp_executesql @sql;
```

In this example, **@sql** is a dynamic SQL string that is constructed based on the value of **@param**. The **sp_executesql** system stored procedure is used to execute the dynamically generated SQL.
Dynamic SQL is powerful but should be used with caution to avoid SQL injection vulnerabilities. Always validate and sanitize user inputs when using dynamic SQL.
Cursors:
A cursor is a database object used to retrieve and manipulate data from a result set one row at a time. Cursors are often used when you need to process rows sequentially, perform calculations, or modify data within a result set.
There are different types of cursors:
Forward-Only Cursor: It allows you to move only forward in the result set and does not support scrolling or going backward.
Static Cursor: It creates a snapshot of the result set when the cursor is opened. Changes in the underlying data are not visible.
Dynamic Cursor: It reflects changes in the underlying data as you scroll through the result set. It allows for updates.
Keyset Cursor: Similar to a dynamic cursor but optimized for larger result sets. It keeps track of the keys of the rows in the result set.
Here's an example of a simple cursor in SQL Server:

```
DECLARE @ID INT;
DECLARE @Name VARCHAR(50);

DECLARE myCursor CURSOR FOR
SELECT ID, Name FROM YourTable;

OPEN myCursor;

FETCH NEXT FROM myCursor INTO @ID, @Name;
WHILE @@FETCH_STATUS = 0
BEGIN
```

```
    -- Process the current row
    PRINT 'ID: ' + CAST(@ID AS VARCHAR(10)) + ', Name: ' + @Name;

    FETCH NEXT FROM myCursor INTO @ID, @Name;
END;

CLOSE myCursor;
DEALLOCATE myCursor;
```

In this example, we declare a cursor, open it, and use it to retrieve and process rows one by one from the result set.

Cursors are powerful, but they should be used judiciously, as they can be less efficient for large result sets and may introduce complexity in your code. In many cases, set-based operations (queries that work with entire result sets) are more efficient than cursors.

Both dynamic SQL and cursors have their use cases in database programming, and their suitability depends on the specific requirements of your application. It's important to choose the right tool for the task to achieve the best performance and maintainability in your database code.

6.5 Exercise

1. What is a stored procedure in MySQL?
a. A temporary table for storing data
b. A function that returns a single value
c. A set of SQL statements that can be executed by calling the procedure
d. A virtual table that combines data from multiple tables
2. What is the primary advantage of using stored procedures in MySQL?
a. Improved data storage efficiency
b. Better data security
c. Enhanced code reusability and maintainability
d. Faster data retrieval
3. In MySQL, how are stored procedures typically executed?
a. By running a SELECT statement
b. By executing a CALL statement
c. By using the INSERT INTO statement
d. By using the CREATE PROCEDURE statement
4. Which of the following is a valid naming convention for stored procedures in MySQL?
a. Starting with a number
b. Containing spaces or special characters
c. Using meaningful and descriptive names
d. Having a maximum length of 10 characters
5. What keyword is used to define the beginning of a stored procedure in MySQL?
a. BEGIN
b. START
c. DECLARE
d. OPEN
6. What is the purpose of the OUT parameter in a MySQL stored procedure?
a. It specifies the input values for the procedure.
b. It defines a variable that receives a value from the procedure.
c. It is used to display output messages.
d. It is used to control the flow of the procedure.
7. How can you drop (delete) a stored procedure in MySQL?
a. Use the DROP PROCEDURE statement.
b. Use the DELETE FROM PROCEDURE statement.
c. Use the ALTER PROCEDURE statement.
d. Use the TRUNCATE PROCEDURE statement.
8. Which of the following SQL statements can be used within a stored procedure in MySQL?
a. SELECT
b. CREATE DATABASE
c. CREATE TABLE
d. SHOW TABLES
9. What is the role of the ROLLBACK statement in a MySQL stored procedure?
a. It starts a new transaction.
b. It commits all changes made by the procedure.

c. It undoes changes made within the current transaction.
d. It retrieves data from the database.
10. Which MySQL client utility can be used to execute a stored procedure from the command line?
a. mysqlimport
b. mysqlshow
c. mysqladmin
d. mysql
11. What is the primary purpose of User-Defined Functions (UDFs) in MySQL?
a. To define table structures
b. To create new databases
c. To extend MySQL's functionality with custom functions
d. To optimize query performance
12. Which programming language is commonly used to create User-Defined Functions (UDFs) in MySQL?
a. Python
b. JavaScript
c. PHP
d. C/C++
13. Which type of User-Defined Function (UDF) can be used to perform calculations and return a single value in MySQL?
a. Scalar UDF
b. Table UDF
c. Stored Procedure
d. Trigger
14. Which of the following statements about UDFs in MySQL is true?
a. UDFs can only be used in SELECT queries.
b. UDFs are built-in MySQL functions.
c. UDFs are created by users to add custom functions to MySQL.
d. UDFs can only return integer values.
15. How can you load a User-Defined Function (UDF) in MySQL?
a. UDFs are automatically loaded when the MySQL server starts.
b. Use the LOAD UDF statement.
c. Use the CREATE FUNCTION statement.
d. UDFs cannot be loaded in MySQL.
16. In MySQL, what is the purpose of a transaction?
a. To handle runtime errors
b. To store and retrieve data
c. To group a sequence of SQL statements into a single, atomic operation
d. To define user roles and permissions
17. What keyword is used to start a transaction in MySQL?
a. BEGIN
b. COMMIT
c. ROLLBACK
d. SAVEPOINT
18. In a transaction, what happens if a ROLLBACK statement is executed?
a. The transaction is saved to the database.
b. All changes made within the transaction are permanently applied to the database.
c. The transaction is cancelled, and all changes made within the transaction are undone.
d. The transaction is completed successfully.
19. Which SQL statement is used to save a setpoint in MySQL for partial transaction rollbacks?
a. BEGIN
b. COMMIT
c. ROLLBACK
d. SAVEPOINT
20. In MySQL, what is the purpose of the ACID properties in transactions?
a. To ensure that transactions are irreversible
b. To define table constraints
c. To guarantee the reliability and integrity of database transactions
d. To control user access to the database
21. What is Dynamic SQL in MySQL?
a. SQL statements generated and executed at runtime

b. SQL statements stored in the database schema
c. SQL statements that cannot be modified
d. SQL statements used for data retrieval

22. When might you use Dynamic SQL in MySQL?
a. To hardcode SQL statements for better performance
b. To execute SQL statements based on variable conditions
c. To restrict the use of SQL statements
d. To perform data indexing

23. Which statement is true about Cursors in MySQL?
a. Cursors are used to manipulate database tables.
b. Cursors are used to store temporary data.
c. Cursors are used to iterate through the result set of a SELECT query.
d. Cursors are not supported in MySQL.

24. What is the primary purpose of a Cursor in MySQL?
a. To enable parallel execution of SQL statements
b. To store large result sets in memory
c. To process individual rows in a result set one at a time
d. To update all rows in a table simultaneously

25. Which type of Cursor in MySQL allows data modification operations?
a. FORWARD-ONLY Cursor
b. SCROLL Cursor
c. READ-ONLY Cursor
d. DYNAMIC Cursor

Answer

1) c. 2) c. 3) b. 4) c. 5) a. 6) b. 7) a. 8) a. 9) c. 10) d. 11) c. 12) d. 13) a. 14) c. 15) b. 16) c. 17) a. 18) c. 19) d. 20) c. 21) a. 22) b. 23) c. 24) c. 25) b. 26) a. 27) c. 28) a. 29) d. 30) b.

ONLINE RESOURCES

Practice Paper
Link: https://forms.gle/wyvunkp4dqdj6ynd7
QR Code:

Video Content:
Link: https://www.youtube.com/playlist?list=PLzlh_31VWEFoNLO-nMGMAO166a_WRC4-0
QR Code:

7.1 Importing and Exporting Data

Importing and exporting data is a common task in database management, often used to transfer data between different databases, backup data, or load data into a database from external sources. The methods and tools for importing and exporting data can vary depending on the database system you are using. Here is a general overview of the process:

Exporting Data:

Exporting data typically involves extracting data from a database and saving it in an external file or in a specific format. Here are common methods and tools for exporting data:

SQL Commands: Most database systems support SQL commands to export data to standard file formats like CSV, TSV, or JSON. For example, in MySQL, you can use the **SELECT INTO OUTFILE** statement to export data to a file:

```
SELECT * INTO OUTFILE '/path/to/file.csv'
FIELDS TERMINATED BY ',' OPTIONALLY ENCLOSED BY '"'
LINES TERMINATED BY '\n'
FROM TableName;
```

Database Backup Tools: Many database systems offer backup utilities that allow you to create full database backups. These backups can include both the schema and the data. Popular backup tools include **mysqldump** for MySQL, **pg_dump** for PostgreSQL, and **sqlcmd** for SQL Server.

ETL (Extract, Transform, Load) Tools: ETL tools like Apache NiFi, Talend, or Apache Spark are used for extracting, transforming, and loading data between different systems. They often include features for exporting data from databases.

Database Export Wizards: Some database management tools, such as phpMyAdmin for MySQL or pgAdmin for PostgreSQL, provide graphical wizards for exporting data.

Importing Data:

Importing data involves loading data into a database from external sources or files. Here are common methods and tools for importing data:

SQL Commands: You can use SQL statements like **LOAD DATA INFILE** (MySQL), **COPY** (PostgreSQL), or **BULK INSERT** (SQL Server) to import data from external files.

Database Restore Tools: Database backup tools often have corresponding restore utilities that allow you to import data from backup files.

ETL Tools: ETL tools can also be used for importing data by defining data transformation and loading processes.

CSV or Other Data Format Import: Many database systems offer the ability to import data from CSV, TSV, XML, or other data formats. You may use graphical tools or command-line utilities to accomplish this.

Custom Scripts or Programs: For complex data imports, you may write custom scripts or programs using programming languages like Python, Java, or PHP to handle data import tasks.

Considerations:

Ensure data compatibility: When exporting and importing data, make sure the data formats and schemas are compatible between the source and destination databases.

Data integrity: Pay attention to data integrity and constraints, especially when importing data. Ensure that imported data adheres to the defined constraints and business rules.

Performance: Data export and import can be resource-intensive operations. Optimize your processes for performance and scalability.

Security: Protect sensitive data during export and import operations, especially when data is moved across different systems or shared externally.

Logging and error handling: Implement logging and error handling mechanisms to track the success or failure of data export and import tasks.

The specific methods and tools you use for data import and export depend on your database system and the nature of your data migration or backup needs. It's essential to choose the right approach for your specific use case and follow best practices to ensure data integrity and security.

7.2 Data Transfer Methods

Data transfer methods refer to the techniques and tools used to move data from one location to another. These methods are essential for tasks such as data migration, data sharing between systems, and data synchronization. There are various data transfer methods available, depending on the source and destination of the data, the volume of data, and other factors. Here are some common data transfer methods:

File Transfer:

File Copy: This method involves copying files or directories from one location to another, either locally or over a network. Common tools include **cp**, **rsync**, **robocopy**, and FTP clients.

Compression and Archiving: Before transferring, data can be compressed and archived using tools like **zip**, **tar**, or **gzip**, making the transfer faster and more efficient.

Database Transfer:

SQL Dump and Restore: For relational databases, you can export data using SQL dump files (e.g., **mysqldump**, **pg_dump**) and then import it into another database using SQL restore commands.

Data Integration Tools: ETL (Extract, Transform, Load) tools like Apache Nifi, Talend, or Apache Spark are used for transferring and transforming data between different databases or systems.
Database Replication: Some databases support replication mechanisms that automatically transfer and synchronize data between multiple instances or databases.
API and Web Services:
API Calls: Many web services and cloud platforms offer APIs for data transfer. You can use HTTP requests to transfer data between systems.
RESTful APIs: RESTful APIs are commonly used for data transfer between web applications, allowing you to perform actions like GET, POST, PUT, and DELETE on resources.
SOAP Web Services: SOAP (Simple Object Access Protocol) is another protocol for transferring structured data between applications.
Data Streaming:
Message Queues: Message queues like Apache Kafka, RabbitMQ, and AWS SQS allow real-time data streaming and transfer between distributed systems.
Streaming Platforms: Stream processing platforms like Apache Kafka Streams, Apache Flink, and Apache Beam are used for real-time data processing and transfer.
Cloud Services:
Cloud Data Transfer Services: Cloud providers offer services (e.g., AWS DataSync, Google Transfer Appliance, Azure Data Box) for transferring large volumes of data to and from the cloud securely.
Data Transfer Services: Services like AWS Data Pipeline, Google Cloud Dataflow, and Azure Data Factory are used for orchestrating and automating data transfer workflows in the cloud.
Network Transfer:
Network Protocols: Data can be transferred between systems using various network protocols, such as FTP, SFTP, SCP, HTTP, and SMB/CIFS.
Remote Copy: Tools like **scp**, **rsync**, and **rsync over SSH** enable secure data transfer over networks.
Cloud Storage and Sync:
Cloud Storage Services: Cloud storage providers like Dropbox, Google Drive, and OneDrive offer synchronized storage for sharing and syncing files across devices.
File Sync Software: Software like Microsoft OneDrive, Dropbox, and rsync can be used for file synchronization.
Physical Transfer:
External Media: In situations where online transfer is impractical, data can be moved physically using external media like hard drives, DVDs, or tapes.
Data Shipment Services: Some cloud providers offer data shipment services where you can physically ship data on storage devices for transfer to the cloud.
Peer-to-Peer (P2P) File Sharing:
BitTorrent: BitTorrent is a P2P file-sharing protocol that allows users to download and share large files directly with others.
The choice of data transfer method depends on various factors, including the nature of the data, security requirements, transfer volume, distance, and available infrastructure. Selecting the appropriate method and tools is essential for ensuring data transfer efficiency and integrity.

7.3 Working with CSV and XML Data

Working with CSV (Comma-Separated Values) and XML (eXtensible Markup Language) data is a common task in data manipulation and integration. Both formats are widely used for storing and exchanging structured data. Here's how to work with CSV and XML data:
Working with CSV Data:
Reading CSV Data:

Python: You can use the built-in **csv** module to read and write CSV files. The **csv.reader** object is used to read CSV data.
R: The **read.csv()** function is commonly used to read CSV files.
Excel: You can open CSV files directly in Microsoft Excel.

Writing CSV Data:

Python: The **csv.writer** object is used to write data to CSV files.
R: The **write.csv()** function is used to save data to a CSV file.
Excel: You can save a spreadsheet as a CSV file in Excel.

Libraries and Tools:

Data Analysis: Libraries like Pandas (Python) and data analysis tools like R and Excel are popular for handling and analyzing CSV data.
ETL (Extract, Transform, Load): ETL tools like Talend and Apache NiFi can handle CSV data transformation and loading.

CSV Processing:

Data Transformation: You can use scripting languages like Python or R to manipulate, clean, and transform CSV data.
Data Integration: ETL tools and data integration platforms can perform complex operations on CSV data.

Working with XML Data:

Parsing XML Data:

Python: The **xml.etree.ElementTree** or **lxml** library is used for parsing XML data.

Java: Libraries like DOM, SAX, and StAX are commonly used for parsing XML in Java.

.NET: The **System.Xml** namespace provides classes for XML parsing in C#.

Creating XML Data:

Python: You can use the same libraries to create and generate XML data.

Java: XML documents can be created using classes from the Java XML API.

.NET: The **System.Xml** namespace allows you to create and manipulate XML documents in C#.

XSLT (eXtensible Stylesheet Language Transformations):

XSLT is used for transforming XML documents into different formats or structures. You can use XSLT processors or libraries to perform transformations.

XPath and XQuery:

XPath and XQuery are query languages for XML data. They are used to extract and manipulate XML data efficiently.

Libraries and Tools:

Data Integration: ETL tools often have components for processing XML data.

XML Databases: XML databases like MarkLogic and BaseX are designed for storing and querying XML data.

XML Processing:

Data Transformation: Use programming languages or tools to transform and clean XML data.

Data Validation: XML Schema or Document Type Definitions (DTDs) can be used to validate XML data.

Web Services:

Many web services use XML for data exchange in the form of SOAP (Simple Object Access Protocol) or RESTful APIs. You can work with XML to interact with these services.

Best Practices for Working with CSV and XML Data:

Data Validation: Always validate the integrity and structure of CSV and XML data before processing. This helps prevent errors and data inconsistencies.

Data Transformation: Use appropriate tools or scripting languages for data transformation and cleaning. This is crucial for ensuring the quality of the data.

Security: Be aware of security considerations when parsing XML data from untrusted sources to prevent XML injection attacks. Properly sanitize and validate data to avoid security vulnerabilities.

Performance: Optimize your code or use efficient libraries to process large CSV and XML datasets, as inefficient code can lead to performance issues.

Documentation: Maintain documentation for XML schemas and data formats to ensure proper handling. Well-documented XML schemas make it easier for others to understand and work with your data.

Testing: Test your data processing code with various data scenarios to ensure reliability and correctness. Data-driven testing is particularly useful in this context.

Working with CSV and XML data is a fundamental skill in data manipulation, integration, and analysis. Depending on your specific use case, you can choose the most suitable tools and programming languages to handle these formats efficiently.

7.4 Backups and Recovery

Backups and recovery are critical components of database management and are essential for ensuring data integrity, availability, and continuity in case of data loss, corruption, or system failures. Here's an overview of backups and recovery in the context of database systems:

Backups:

Types of Backups:

Full Backup: A full backup contains a complete copy of the entire database. It's the most comprehensive type of backup.

Differential Backup: A differential backup contains all the changes made since the last full backup. It's smaller than a full backup but larger than an incremental backup.

Incremental Backup: An incremental backup contains only the changes made since the last backup, which can be either a full or differential backup.

Backup Strategies:

Regular Backups: Implement a backup schedule that suits your data's criticality and the frequency of changes. Common schedules include daily, weekly, or monthly backups.

Automated Backups: Use backup automation tools or features provided by database systems to streamline the backup process.

Offsite Backups: Store backups in a different location to protect against disasters like fires or floods. Cloud-based backup services are popular for this purpose.

Database Snapshot: Some database systems support database snapshots, which are read-only copies of the database at a specific point in time. Snapshots are useful for data consistency and reporting.

Transaction Logs: Transaction logs record all changes made to a database. They are critical for point-in-time recovery and are included in backup strategies.

Recovery:

Data Restoration:

- **Restoring Full Backups:** In case of a complete data loss, you can restore the most recent full backup, followed by the application of differential and incremental backups, if available.
- **Point-in-Time Recovery:** Transaction logs are essential for point-in-time recovery. You can restore a database to a specific moment in time, using transaction logs to roll forward or backward.

Recovery Plans:

- **Disaster Recovery Plan:** Develop a comprehensive plan for recovering data in the event of a disaster. Include procedures, roles, responsibilities, and communication strategies.
- **Backup Validation:** Regularly test your backups to ensure they are valid and can be restored successfully.

High Availability and Failover:

- Implement high availability solutions such as clustering, mirroring, or replication to ensure minimal downtime in case of hardware or software failures.
- Database failover mechanisms automatically switch to a standby server to maintain service continuity.

Backup Encryption: To enhance security, use backup encryption to protect data at rest during backups.

Backup Retention: Define a backup retention policy to determine how long backup files are stored. Consider compliance and regulatory requirements.

Monitoring and Alerting: Implement monitoring and alerting systems to promptly detect issues and initiate the recovery process.

Data Corruption Handling: Plan for the possibility of data corruption and implement strategies for identifying and recovering from data corruption.

Documentation: Maintain documentation of your backup and recovery processes, including recovery steps, contact information, and configurations.

Best Practices:

Regularly Test Backups: Ensure backups are tested and validated to guarantee that they can be restored successfully.

Offsite and Cloud Backups: Store backups in an offsite location, such as cloud storage, for disaster recovery.

Automate Backups: Implement automated backup routines to reduce the risk of human error.

Consistent Naming Conventions: Use consistent and clear naming conventions for backup files and directories.

Education and Training: Ensure that your team is trained in backup and recovery procedures.

Regularly Review and Update Strategies: Review your backup and recovery strategies periodically to accommodate changing data requirements and technologies.

Security Measures: Protect backups with encryption and access controls to prevent unauthorized access and data breaches.

Recovery Point and Time Objectives (RPO and RTO): Determine and communicate acceptable levels for data loss (RPO) and downtime (RTO).

Regular Audits: Conduct audits and drills to assess the effectiveness of your backup and recovery procedures.

Backup and recovery are essential for data preservation and business continuity. Implementing robust strategies and regularly testing your recovery processes will help ensure that your data remains secure and accessible in all circumstances.

7.5 Exercise

1. What is the purpose of importing and exporting data in MySQL?

a. To create new tables in the database
b. To copy an entire database to another server
c. To transfer data between MySQL and non-MySQL databases
d. To optimize query performance

2. Which statement is used to import data from an SQL dump file in MySQL?

a. IMPORT DATA
b. LOAD DATA INFILE
c. IMPORT FILE
d. RESTORE DATABASE

3. What is the file format commonly used for exporting MySQL data?

a. .TXT
b. .CSV
c. .SQL
d. .XLS

4. Which MySQL command is used to export a database into an SQL dump file?

a. EXPORT DATABASE
b. DUMP DATABASE
c. BACKUP DATABASE
d. mysqldump

5. In MySQL, which tool can be used to import and export data as well as synchronize data between databases?

a. mysqldump
b. phpMyAdmin

c. MySQL Workbench
d. MySQL Server Manager
6. When exporting data using mysqldump, which option is used to include the database's structure (tables, indexes) in the dump?
a. --no-create-info
b. --no-data
c. --structure-only
d. --no-structure
7. Which statement is used to import data from a CSV file into a MySQL table?
a. IMPORT DATA
b.LOAD DATA INFILE
c. INSERT DATA
d. IMPORT TABLE
8. What is the purpose of the "FIELDS TERMINATED BY" clause in a LOAD DATA INFILE statement?
a. It specifies the path to the CSV file.
b. It defines the character that separates fields in the CSV file.
c. It specifies the name of the target table.
d. It defines the database connection parameters.
9. Which MySQL utility can be used to transfer data between a MySQL database and other data sources, such as Excel or XML files?
a. mysqldump
b. mysqlimport
c. Data Transfer Wizard
d. MySQL Connector
10. In MySQL Workbench, what is the purpose of the "Data Export" wizard?
a. To import data from external sources
b. To visualize database schemas
c. To create complex queries
d. To export data to various formats
11. Which statement is used to export data from a MySQL table into a CSV file?
a. EXPORT DATA
b. SELECT INTO OUTFILE
c. BACKUP DATA
d. EXPORT TABLE
12. Which of the following is not a valid file format for data import/export in MySQL?
a. .CSV
b. .SQL
c. .XLS
d. .TXT
13. What is the purpose of the "FIELDS ENCLOSED BY" clause in a LOAD DATA INFILE statement?
a. It specifies the name of the target table.
b. It defines the character that encloses fields in the CSV file.
c. It specifies the path to the CSV file.
d. It defines the database connection parameters.
14. In MySQL, which utility can be used for bulk data loading and importing from text files?
a. mysqldump
b. mysqlimport
c. Data Transfer Manager
d. MySQL Connector
15. Which statement is used to export a MySQL table structure (without data) into an SQL dump file?
a. mysqldump --no-data
b. EXPORT DATABASE
c. DUMP DATABASE
d. BACKUP DATABASE
16. Which statement is true when working with CSV data in MySQL?
a. CSV files cannot be imported into MySQL.
b. MySQL provides the LOAD DATA INFILE statement for importing CSV data.
c. MySQL can only export data to CSV but not import from it.
d. CSV data is automatically converted to XML when imported into MySQL.
17. In MySQL, what does the term "XML" stand for?
a. eXtensible Markup Language
b. Extended MySQL Language
c. Extract, Modify, Load
d. Extraordinary Markup Layer

18. Which statement is true about exporting data as XML from MySQL?
a. MySQL does not support exporting data as XML.
b. You can use the SELECT INTO XML statement to export data in XML format.
c. XML export is only available in the Enterprise edition of MySQL.
d. XML export can only be done via a third-party tool.
19. When importing data from a CSV file, which clause is used in the LOAD DATA INFILE statement to specify the file path and format?
a. FILE
b. FROM
c. INTO
d. IN
20. Which MySQL command is used to export query results to a CSV file?
a. EXPORT TO CSV
b. SELECT INTO CSV
c. SELECT ... INTO OUTFILE
d. EXPORT AS CSV
21. What is a full backup in MySQL?
a. It backs up all the data in the database.
b. It only backs up the schema, not the data.
c. It is a backup of transaction logs.
d. It is a backup of a specific table.
22. Which statement is true regarding MySQL binary logs?
a. They are used for full database backups.
b. They contain a record of all changes to the database.
c. They can only be used for replication purposes.
d. They are not related to backups.
23. What is the purpose of the mysqldump utility in MySQL?
a. To load data into MySQL.
b. To perform partial backups of specific tables.
c. To restore a database to a previous state.
d. To create binary log files.
24. Which MySQL storage engine supports hot backups?
a. InnoDB
b. MyISAM
c. MEMORY
d. NDB
25. Which statement is true about point-in-time recovery in MySQL?
a. It allows you to recover data to any arbitrary point in time.
b. It can only recover data to the last full backup.
c. It is not supported in MySQL.
d. It requires stopping the MySQL server during recovery.
26. What is the purpose of the FLUSH LOGS statement in MySQL?
a. To clear the binary log files.
b. To flush the query cache.
c. To terminate all active connections.
d. To optimize the database tables.
27. Which MySQL utility is used for physical backups and is typically used with the InnoDB storage engine?
a. mysqldump
b. mysqlbinlog
c. xtrabackup
d. mysqlhotcopy
28. Which backup method is the fastest but may lock the database during the backup process?
a. Logical backup
b. Physical backup
c. Binary backup
d. Cold backup
29. What is a cold backup in MySQL?
a. A backup taken while the database is running.
b. A backup taken when the server is offline.
c. A backup that includes only the data and not the schema.
d. A backup taken in XML format.
30. In MySQL, what is the purpose of the binary log purge process?
a. To create binary log files.
b. To restore data from binary logs.

c. To automatically delete outdated binary log files.
d. To analyze query performance.

Answer

1) c. 2) b. 3) b. 4) d. 5) c. 6) d. 7) b. 8) b. 9) b. 10) d. 11) b. 12) c. 13) b. 14) b. 15) a. 16) b. 17) a. 18) b. 19) b. 20) c. 21) a. 22) b. 23) b. 24) a. 25) a. 26) a. 27) c. 28) d. 29) b. 30) c.

ONLINE RESOURCES

Practice Paper
Link: https://forms.gle/fzBocJDGJ32dZ1MJA
QR Code:

Video Content:
Link: https://www.youtube.com/playlist?list=PLzlh_31VWEFp5Ra5jTT_FKmdDPILuwN05
QR Code:

8.1 Query Optimization Techniques

Query optimization in MySQL is a crucial aspect of improving the performance of your database system. When you work with large datasets and complex queries, optimizing SQL queries can make a significant difference in response times. Here are some detailed query optimization techniques in MySQL:

Use Indexes:

Indexes are data structures that speed up data retrieval operations. Ensure that the columns you frequently filter, join, or sort by are appropriately indexed.

Use composite indexes (indexes on multiple columns) when necessary. However, be mindful of over-indexing, as it can lead to increased storage and maintenance costs.

Analyze and Optimize Queries:

Use MySQL's **EXPLAIN** statement to analyze query execution plans. This helps identify slow-performing parts of a query and allows you to optimize them.

Review the output of **EXPLAIN** to check for full table scans, inefficient joins, and potential index usage.

Avoid SELECT:

Specify only the columns you need in the **SELECT** statement. Using **SELECT *** retrieves all columns and can result in unnecessary data transfer and processing.

Minimize Subqueries and JOINs:

Subqueries and JOINs can be resource-intensive. Whenever possible, try to replace them with more efficient queries or temporary tables.

Use **JOIN** conditions that minimize the number of rows involved in the join operation.

Use Appropriate Data Types:

Choose the most appropriate data types for your columns. Smaller data types consume less space and improve query performance.

For example, use **INT** instead of **VARCHAR** for integer values.

Avoid Wildcard Searches:

Searches that start with wildcard characters (**%**) can't utilize indexes efficiently. If possible, structure your queries to avoid leading wildcards.

Consider using full-text search for complex text searching needs.

Partitioning:

MySQL supports table partitioning, which can improve query performance for large tables by dividing them into smaller, more manageable partitions.

Partitioning can be beneficial for range-based queries on time-series data or other partitioning criteria.

Cache Query Results:

Use MySQL's query cache to store and reuse the results of frequently executed queries.

However, be cautious with query caching for high-write workloads, as it can lead to cache invalidation issues.

Tune the Buffer Pool:

Adjust the InnoDB buffer pool size to accommodate the working dataset in memory. This reduces disk I/O, improving query response times.

Monitor and analyze memory usage to fine-tune this setting.

Database and Table Normalization:

Normalize your database schema to eliminate redundancy and improve data consistency.

However, don't over-normalize, as it can lead to complex and slow JOIN operations.

Avoid Using Functions in WHERE Clauses:

Using functions in **WHERE** clauses can prevent MySQL from using indexes. Whenever possible, apply functions to columns rather than the other way around.

For instance, instead of **WHERE DATE_FORMAT(date_column, '%Y-%m-%d') = '2023-10-01'**, use **WHERE date_column = '2023-10-01'**.

Limit the Result Set:

Use the **LIMIT** clause to restrict the number of rows returned by a query. This can significantly reduce query execution time, especially for paginated results.

Additionally, consider pagination using keyset pagination for large result sets.

Database Server Configuration:

Adjust MySQL server configuration parameters, such as **innodb_buffer_pool_size**, **key_buffer_size**, and **query_cache_size**, based on your system's resources and workload.

Regularly Update Statistics:

Keep table statistics up-to-date using the **ANALYZE TABLE** command to help the query planner make better decisions.

Profiling and Benchmarking:

Use profiling tools to identify bottlenecks and performance issues in your queries.

Benchmark your queries under various conditions to understand their performance characteristics.

Caching:

Implement application-level caching to store query results, reducing the load on the database for frequently accessed data.

Horizontal Partitioning:

If your data volume is too high, consider horizontal partitioning (splitting tables into smaller tables based on specific criteria) to improve query performance.

Use Stored Procedures and Prepared Statements:

Stored procedures and prepared statements can reduce query parsing overhead and enhance security. Parameters in prepared statements are sent separately from the SQL, reducing the risk of SQL injection.

Query Rewriting:

Analyze complex queries and see if they can be rewritten in a more efficient way. Sometimes, restructuring the query can lead to significant performance improvements.

Update MySQL Version:

Ensure that you are using a reasonably recent version of MySQL. Newer versions often come with performance improvements and bug fixes, so keeping your database software up to date can lead to better query optimization.

Monitoring and Profiling Tools:

Use monitoring and profiling tools like MySQL Performance Schema, MySQL Enterprise Monitor, or third-party tools to gain insights into query performance and identify areas for optimization.

InnoDB Buffer Pool Warm-up:

InnoDB is the default storage engine for MySQL. Consider warming up the InnoDB buffer pool by running read-only queries or a specific set of queries that mimic the typical workload. This helps keep frequently accessed data in memory.

Connection Pooling:

Implement connection pooling to manage and reuse database connections efficiently. This reduces the overhead of establishing and tearing down connections for each query.

Query Rewrite Plugins:

MySQL offers the ability to create custom query rewrite plugins. These plugins can help you optimize and transform queries based on your specific requirements.

Avoid Complex Expressions in SELECT Lists:

Avoid using complex expressions or functions in the **SELECT** list. These can slow down query execution. If needed, calculate complex expressions in application code.

Use Application-Side Caching:

Implement caching at the application level, using tools like Memcached or Redis, to cache query results and reduce the load on the database.

Consider Sharding:

For extremely large datasets, consider sharding, which involves splitting the data into smaller, distributed databases or servers. Sharding can help distribute the query load.

Concurrency Control:

Carefully choose the appropriate level of concurrency control, such as the isolation level in your transactions. Using overly strict isolation levels can lead to contention and slow query performance.

Avoid Using ORDER BY RAND():

Sorting results using **ORDER BY RAND()** can be very slow for large datasets. Consider alternative methods to randomize query results.

Regular Database Maintenance:

Perform regular database maintenance tasks, such as optimizing and repairing tables, as they can help improve query performance over time.

Query-Level and Index-Level Hints:

Use query hints (e.g., **STRAIGHT_JOIN**) and index hints (e.g., **USE INDEX**, **FORCE INDEX**) to influence query execution plans when necessary.

Resource Scaling:

Consider scaling your hardware resources, such as CPU, RAM, and storage, to handle query workloads more efficiently.

Database Partitioning:

For large tables, partitioning can significantly improve query performance by distributing data across multiple physical or logical partitions.

MySQL's Query Cache:

Although query caching can help, be cautious when enabling the query cache. It's not always beneficial and may not work well in high-write workloads.

Query and Schema Optimization Tools:

Explore third-party tools and services designed for query and schema optimization. Some tools can provide automated suggestions and improvements.

Remember that query optimization is an ongoing process. Continuously monitor query performance, analyze execution plans, and apply optimization techniques as needed to adapt to changing data volumes and query patterns. Each application and database environment may require a tailored approach to achieve the best performance.

8.2 Indexing Strategies

Indexing is a crucial aspect of database optimization in MySQL. Indexes improve query performance by allowing the database engine to quickly locate and retrieve data. Here are detailed indexing strategies and best practices in MySQL:

Understanding Indexes:

Primary Key Index: Every InnoDB table should have a primary key. By default, the primary key is indexed. It uniquely identifies each row in the table.

Unique Index: A unique index enforces the uniqueness of values in one or more columns. It can be applied to ensure data integrity.

Non-Unique Index: Non-unique indexes speed up data retrieval but do not enforce data uniqueness.

Composite Index: An index on multiple columns, known as a composite index, can improve query performance for conditions that involve those columns.

Full-Text Index: Full-text indexes are used for text-based searching, enabling efficient searching of large text fields.

Choosing Columns to Index:

Frequently Filtered Columns: Index columns that are frequently used in the **WHERE** clause of your queries.

Foreign Keys: Index foreign key columns to speed up JOIN operations.

Columns in JOIN and ORDER BY: Columns used in **JOIN** operations and **ORDER BY** clauses benefit from indexing.

Columns with Range Conditions: Index columns involved in range conditions, such as date ranges, to speed up data retrieval.

MySQL Storage Engines:

Different storage engines in MySQL handle indexes differently. InnoDB is the most commonly used storage engine for its support of ACID transactions, while MyISAM uses a simpler index structure.

InnoDB tables should have a primary key, as InnoDB clusters data rows based on the primary key.

Indexing Large Text Columns:

For large text columns, consider using a full-text index or using an external search engine like Elasticsearch for text-based searches. Full-text indexing in MySQL is most effective for small to medium-sized text fields.

Index Length:

In MySQL, you can specify the length for index keys, which can be particularly useful for improving query performance on long text or VARCHAR columns.

Index length should be chosen wisely to balance between query performance and storage space.

Index Prefixing:

For composite indexes, you can use index prefixing by creating an index on only the leftmost part of the column. This can be efficient when queries use only a prefix of the indexed column.

Be cautious about index prefixing, as it can lead to index merging and might not improve performance as expected.

Multi-Column Indexes:

When creating indexes on multiple columns, carefully consider the order of columns in the index. Put columns used for equality conditions first and those used for range conditions later.

Index Hints:

Use query hints like **USE INDEX** and **FORCE INDEX** to suggest specific indexes to the MySQL query optimizer for individual queries when you know that certain indexes should be used.

Query Optimization:

Analyze your queries and execution plans using the **EXPLAIN** statement. This helps identify inefficient queries and the use of indexes.

Use query profiling to measure the time taken by different parts of a query, which can help in pinpointing performance bottlenecks.

Indexing and Performance Considerations:

Be mindful of the trade-offs between query performance and write operations. Indexes can slow down insert, update, and delete operations.

Periodically reorganize and optimize indexes, especially if your data distribution or query patterns change significantly.

Statistics and Optimization:

MySQL maintains statistics on index cardinality and distribution, which the query optimizer uses to generate query execution plans. Ensure that these statistics are up-to-date for accurate optimization.

Partitioning:

Partitioning can be an advanced strategy for handling very large tables. It divides a table into smaller, more manageable partitions, each with its own index.

Indexing on Virtual Columns:

MySQL supports the creation of indexes on virtual (generated) columns. These columns are computed based on expressions or operations on other columns.

Index Size and Storage:

Be aware of the storage requirements for indexes. Larger indexes can lead to increased storage usage and may impact performance.

Review and Monitor:

Regularly review your indexing strategies and monitor the performance of your queries. Be ready to adjust and optimize indexes as the application evolves.

SQL Modes and Index Behavior:

MySQL's SQL modes can affect indexing behavior. Some modes change how MySQL handles NULL values in indexed columns or the handling of values that exceed the column's data type limits.

Optimizing indexing in MySQL requires a deep understanding of your application's query patterns and data distribution. It's essential to strike a balance between read and write operations and to regularly monitor and fine-tune your indexing strategy to ensure optimal database performance.

8.3 Profiling and Benchmarking

Profiling and benchmarking are essential practices in MySQL database administration and development. They help you identify performance bottlenecks, optimize queries, and ensure your database runs efficiently. Below, I'll explain profiling and benchmarking in MySQL in detail:

Profiling in MySQL:

Profiling involves measuring and analyzing the performance of SQL queries to identify areas for improvement. MySQL provides built-in tools to help with profiling:

Query Profiling:

MySQL allows you to profile a specific query using the **SHOW PROFILE** statement. This provides detailed information about the query's execution, including the duration of each stage (e.g., parsing, optimization, execution).

```
SET profiling = 1; -- Your SQL query here SHOW PROFILES; SHOW PROFILE FOR QUERY 1;
```

Query Execution Plan:

Use **EXPLAIN** to obtain the execution plan for a query. It provides insights into how MySQL processes the query, including the chosen indexes, join types, and estimated row counts.

```
EXPLAIN SELECT * FROM your_table WHERE column = 'value';
```

Performance Schema:

MySQL's Performance Schema is a powerful feature for query performance analysis. It provides detailed statistics on query execution, resource consumption, and more. You can query Performance Schema tables to obtain valuable insights.

```
SELECT * FROM performance_schema.events_statements_summary_by_digest;
```

SHOW VARIABLES and SHOW STATUS:

MySQL provides various server variables and status information that can be queried to monitor the database's performance. These include variables like **innodb_buffer_pool_size** and status values like **Threads_connected**.

```
SHOW VARIABLES LIKE 'innodb_buffer_pool_size'; SHOW STATUS LIKE 'Threads_connected';
```

Benchmarking in MySQL:

Benchmarking involves testing the performance of your MySQL database under different conditions, workloads, and configurations. It helps you assess how your database handles various scenarios and identify potential performance bottlenecks:

SysBench:

SysBench is a popular MySQL benchmarking tool. It can simulate various database workloads, including read-heavy and write-heavy scenarios, to assess database performance.

Example to test CPU performance:

```
sysbench cpu --cpu-max-prime=20000 run
```

TPC Benchmarks:

The Transaction Processing Performance Council (TPC) provides standardized benchmarks for measuring the performance of database systems. You can use TPC-C, TPC-H, or other benchmarks to evaluate your MySQL database's performance.

Custom Workload Scripts:

Create custom scripts to simulate your application's workloads. These scripts can include a mix of SELECT, INSERT, UPDATE, and DELETE queries to evaluate real-world scenarios.

Load Testing Tools:

Use load testing tools like Apache JMeter, Apache ab, or Siege to simulate concurrent user traffic and assess how your MySQL database handles increased load.

Best Practices for Profiling and Benchmarking:

Use a Representative Dataset: Benchmarking with a dataset that closely resembles your production data is crucial for realistic results.

Isolate Factors: Isolate the factor you want to test or profile, whether it's a specific query, server configuration, or workload.

Repeat Tests: Run multiple iterations of your tests to account for variations and ensure accuracy in results.

Measure and Analyze: Collect and analyze metrics, such as query execution times, resource utilization, and throughput, to identify performance issues.

Optimize and Re-test: After identifying performance bottlenecks through profiling and benchmarking, make necessary optimizations, such as query rewriting, indexing, or server configuration changes. Then, re-test to ensure improvements.

Document Results: Document your benchmarking and profiling results, including the test conditions and outcomes, for future reference.

Consider Real-World Scenarios: Benchmarking should reflect real-world conditions and query patterns to provide insights into your application's actual performance.

Automate Benchmarking: Automate your benchmarking and profiling processes to conduct tests regularly and under different conditions.

Profiling and benchmarking are essential steps in maintaining a high-performance MySQL database. By identifying and addressing performance issues early, you can ensure that your database meets the demands of your application, even as it grows and evolves.

8.4 Monitoring and Optimization Tools

Monitoring and optimization tools in MySQL are essential for database administrators and developers to maintain and enhance the performance, reliability, and security of MySQL databases. Here is a list of some popular MySQL monitoring and optimization tools:

Monitoring Tools:

MySQL Enterprise Monitor:

MySQL Enterprise Monitor is a commercial monitoring tool offered by Oracle. It provides real-time monitoring, query performance analysis, and alerting for MySQL databases.

Percona Monitoring and Management (PMM):

PMM is an open-source monitoring and management platform for MySQL, MariaDB, and MongoDB. It offers performance monitoring, query analytics, and various database management features.

Prometheus and Grafana:

These open-source tools can be combined to create a powerful monitoring and alerting system for MySQL. Prometheus collects metrics, and Grafana provides visualization and alerting capabilities.

Zabbix:

Zabbix is a versatile open-source monitoring system that can be configured to monitor MySQL databases. It offers a range of notification methods and visualization options.

Nagios:

Nagios is another open-source monitoring system that can be extended with plugins to monitor MySQL database performance and availability.

New Relic:

New Relic offers application performance monitoring (APM) that includes MySQL database monitoring. It provides detailed insights into query performance and database bottlenecks.

Optimization Tools:

MySQL Workbench:

MySQL Workbench is a graphical tool provided by Oracle that offers query performance tuning, schema optimization, and server administration features.

pt-query-digest (Percona Toolkit):

This command-line tool is part of the Percona Toolkit and is used for analyzing and profiling MySQL queries. It helps identify slow queries and potential performance bottlenecks.

MySQLTuner:

MySQLTuner is a Perl script that provides recommendations for optimizing a MySQL server's configuration based on its current usage and performance.

phpMyAdmin Advisor:

phpMyAdmin, a popular web-based MySQL administration tool, includes an Advisor feature that analyzes the database schema and offers optimization suggestions.

Query Profiling with EXPLAIN:

MySQL provides the **EXPLAIN** statement, which can be used to analyze the execution plan of queries. It helps identify inefficiencies in query execution.

SysBench:

SysBench, mentioned in a previous response, can be used for benchmarking and performance testing. It helps identify performance bottlenecks in MySQL.

Backup and Restore Tools:

mysqldump:

MySQL's built-in **mysqldump** tool is used for creating backups of MySQL databases and can also be used for data transfer.

Percona XtraBackup:

Percona XtraBackup is an open-source tool that performs hot backups of MySQL databases. It's especially useful for large databases and high-traffic systems.

MySQL Enterprise Backup:

This is a commercial backup tool from Oracle that offers advanced backup and recovery options, including partial backups and point-in-time recovery.

Security and Vulnerability Scanning:

MySQL Enterprise Security:

MySQL Enterprise Security provides advanced security features, including authentication, encryption, and auditing capabilities, to protect your MySQL databases.

OpenVAS:

OpenVAS is an open-source vulnerability scanner that can be used to identify security vulnerabilities in MySQL databases and associated components.

Nessus:

Nessus is a commercial vulnerability scanner that offers comprehensive security scanning for MySQL and other database systems.

Log Analysis Tools:

Log File Analyzers:

Tools like the ELK Stack (Elasticsearch, Logstash, and Kibana) or Graylog can be used to collect, analyze, and visualize MySQL log data for performance and security insights.

These tools offer a range of features for monitoring, optimizing, securing, and maintaining MySQL databases. The choice of tools depends on your specific requirements, budget, and whether you prefer open-source or commercial solutions. Combining multiple tools may be necessary to cover all aspects of MySQL database management effectively.

8.5 Exercise

1. What is query optimization in MySQL?
a. A process of selecting the most efficient query from a set of possible queries.
b. A process of converting a query into machine code.
c. A process of creating indexes for all columns in a table.
d. A process of generating random queries for testing.
2. Which of the following is a common query optimization technique in MySQL?
a. Caching the entire database in memory.
b. Using appropriate indexes.
c. Running all queries concurrently.
d. Avoiding SQL statements.
3. What is the purpose of an index in a MySQL database?
a. To store all the data in a table.
b. To speed up data retrieval by providing a quick lookup of rows.
c. To encrypt data for security.
d. To create a copy of the table.
4. Which type of index is commonly used in MySQL for primary key and unique key constraints?
a. B-tree index
b. Hash index
c. Full-text index
d. Spatial index
5. When should you use a full-text index in MySQL?
a. For indexing primary keys.
b. For indexing columns with unique constraints.
c. For optimizing text-based search queries.
d. Full-text indexing is not supported in MySQL.
6. What is the primary benefit of using covering indexes in MySQL?
a. They cover the entire table with data.
b. They reduce the storage space required for indexes.
c. They can satisfy a query entirely from the index without accessing the table data.
d. They improve the security of the database.
7. In MySQL, which command is used to analyze the query execution plan?
a. EXPLAIN
b. ANALYZE
c. OPTIMIZE
d. QUERY_PLAN
8. Which storage engine in MySQL is well-suited for applications that require full-text search capabilities?
a. InnoDB
b. MyISAM
c. MEMORY
d. NDB
9. What is an index hint in MySQL?
a. A suggestion for the query optimizer to use a specific index for a query.
b. An index that only contains hints.
c. A type of full-text index.
d. An index that hints at the data structure of a table.
10. What is query caching in MySQL?

a. A technique for storing frequently used queries in a cache for faster retrieval.
b. A way to encrypt queries for security.
c. A method for optimizing query execution plans.
d. A process of storing data in an index.
11. Which of the following statements about index cardinality is true?
a. Index cardinality is always the same as the number of rows in the table.
b. High cardinality means that the index has many distinct values.
c. Low cardinality means that the index is not useful.
d. Index cardinality is not related to query optimization.
12. What is the purpose of the MySQL Query Cache?
a. To cache query execution plans.
b. To cache table data.
c. To cache query results.
d. To cache index definitions.
13. Which MySQL command is used to check the fragmentation of indexes in a table?
a. CHECK TABLE
b. OPTIMIZE TABLE
c. CHECK INDEXES
d. ANALYZE INDEX
14. In MySQL, what is the purpose of the "USE INDEX" query hint?
a. To force the use of a specific index in a query.
b. To create a new index on the table.
c. To clear the query cache.
d. To optimize the query execution plan.
15. When should you avoid using indexes in MySQL?
a. Always use indexes for all columns.
b. For columns with low selectivity (many duplicate values).
c. When you want to slow down query performance.
d. Indexes should never be avoided.
16. What is the primary purpose of profiling in MySQL?
a. To optimize database queries
b. To create new user profiles
c. To encrypt data
d. To delete records
17. Which MySQL command is used for enabling the query profiler for a session?
a. PROFILE ON
b. ENABLE PROFILER
c. SET profiling = 1;
d. START ROFILING;
18. What type of information does MySQL's query profiler provide?
a. Execution time and resource usage for each query
b. User credentials and access control information
c. Server hardware specifications
d. Index statistics for tables
19. Which tool is commonly used for benchmarking MySQL performance by generating a load on the database?
a. MySQL Workbench
b. Apache Benchmark (ab)
c. phpMyAdmin
d. MySQL Query Analyzer
20. What is query benchmarking in MySQL?
a. Measuring query performance and resource usage
b. Running queries in parallel
c. Setting up query subscriptions
d. Profiling user activity
21. What is the primary purpose of the MySQL Performance Schema?
a. To store database schema information
b. To monitor and collect performance-related data
c. To manage user privileges
d. To create triggers and stored procedures

22. Which MySQL tool allows you to view and analyze server status variables and performance metrics?
a. phpMyAdmin
b. MySQL Performance Schema
c. MySQL Enterprise Monitor
d. SHOW STATUS command
23. Which MySQL tool provides a visual interface for query analysis and performance tuning?
a. MySQL Workbench
b. MySQL Shell
c. MySQL Performance Schema
d. mysqldump
24. What does the MySQL EXPLAIN statement provide when analyzing queries?
a. The estimated execution plan for a query
b. The actual execution time for a query
c. User login information
d. The database schema diagram
25. What is the purpose of the MySQL slow query log?
a. To record queries that take longer than a specified time to execute
b. To log all queries, regardless of their execution time
c. To record only successful queries
d. To record queries with syntax errors
26. Which MySQL tool is used for real-time monitoring and alerts for database performance and security?
a. MySQL Performance Schema
b. MySQL Enterprise Monitor
c. MySQL Query Analyzer
d. MySQL Router

Answer

1) a. 2) b. 3) b. 4) a. 5) c. 6) c. 7) a. 8) b. 9) a. 10) a. 11) b. 12) c. 13) b. 14) a. 15) b. 16) a. 17) c. 18) a. 19) b. 20) a. 21) b. 22) d. 23) a. 24) a. 25) a. 26) b. 27) c. 28) d. 29) c. 30) a.

ONLINE RESOURCES

Practice Paper
Link: https://forms.gle/UqdFjaAx5v1w6ctw8
QR Code:

Video Content:
Link: https://www.youtube.com/playlist?list=PLzlh_31VWEFpAYiYYNVrSqr7hsrIcxSSO
QR Code:

Chapter 9: High Availability and Replication

9.1 Introduction to High Availability

High availability (HA) in MySQL refers to a set of practices and technologies designed to ensure that a MySQL database remains accessible and operational, even in the face of hardware failures, software crashes, network issues, or other forms of disruption. The goal of implementing high availability in MySQL is to minimize downtime and data loss, thereby ensuring continuous and reliable access to the database for applications and users.

Here's an introduction to high availability in MySQL:

Key Concepts and Components:

Redundancy: High availability solutions typically involve redundant components, such as multiple database servers, network connections, and storage systems. Redundancy ensures that if one component fails, another can take over seamlessly.

Load Balancing: Load balancers distribute incoming database traffic across multiple servers to ensure even load distribution and to prevent overloading of a single server.

Failover: Failover mechanisms automatically switch database operations to a backup server in case the primary server fails. This process is often transparent to users and applications.

Replication: MySQL supports various replication mechanisms, such as master-slave replication and group replication. Replication involves copying data from one MySQL server to another, creating redundancy and allowing for read scaling.

Clustering: Clustering is a high availability technique where multiple MySQL servers are interconnected to work together as a single logical database. This approach can offer improved performance and failover capabilities.

Challenges Addressed by High Availability:

Downtime Minimization: High availability aims to minimize unplanned downtime due to server or network failures, database crashes, or maintenance tasks.

Data Protection: Redundancy and replication mechanisms protect data against loss. In the event of hardware failure, data remains accessible.

Scalability: High availability solutions often enable horizontal scaling, where additional servers can be added to handle increased traffic and workloads.

Geographic Redundancy: Some high availability configurations involve replicating data across geographically distributed data centers to protect against regional disasters.

High Availability Strategies:

MySQL Replication: MySQL supports master-slave and group replication. In master-slave replication, one server (the master) replicates data to one or more slave servers, providing read scalability and redundancy. Group replication enables multi-master setups for high availability.

Load Balancing: Implement load balancers to distribute read and write queries across multiple MySQL servers. Tools like HAProxy and MySQL Router are commonly used for load balancing.

Failover Clustering: MySQL failover clustering solutions like Percona XtraDB Cluster and MariaDB Galera Cluster provide synchronous multi-master replication and automated failover.

Database Sharding: Sharding involves partitioning data across multiple database servers. It is a technique used for distributing large datasets and achieving scalability and fault tolerance.

Cloud-Based Solutions: Cloud providers offer managed database services with built-in high availability, automated backups, and scaling options. Examples include Amazon RDS and Google Cloud SQL.

Shared Storage Solutions: Use network-attached storage (NAS) or storage area network (SAN) solutions to provide shared, fault-tolerant storage for MySQL servers.

Considerations for High Availability:

Performance Impact: High availability solutions may introduce some performance overhead due to replication, synchronization, and failover mechanisms. Careful planning and monitoring are necessary to optimize performance.

Complexity: Implementing high availability can be complex, involving multiple components and configurations. It's essential to have a clear understanding of the chosen solution.

Data Consistency: In multi-master replication scenarios, ensuring data consistency and avoiding conflicts requires careful application design and transaction management.

Testing and Maintenance: Regular testing and maintenance are critical to ensure that high availability configurations work as intended. Consider periodic failover testing and backup validation.

Cost: High availability solutions may involve additional hardware, software, and operational costs. Consider the trade-offs between cost and the benefits of uptime and data protection.

High availability in MySQL is a fundamental aspect of building robust, mission-critical applications and services. By implementing the right high availability strategy, you can ensure that your MySQL database remains accessible, resilient, and capable of meeting the demands of your applications and users.

9.2 Setting Up Master-Slave Replication

Setting up master-slave replication in MySQL allows you to create a redundant copy of your database on a secondary server, referred to as the slave. This setup provides high availability, read scaling, and data redundancy. Here are the steps to set up master-slave replication in MySQL:

Prerequisites:

Before you start, make sure you have:
Two MySQL servers: One to act as the master and the other as the slave.
Root or administrative access to both servers.
MySQL installed and configured on both servers.

Configure the Master Server:

On the master server, perform the following steps:

Configure MySQL Server:

Edit the MySQL configuration file (my.cnf or my.ini) on the master server to enable binary logging. Open the configuration file and add the following lines under the **[mysqld]** section:

```
server-id = 1  # A unique server ID for the master
log_bin = /var/log/mysql/mysql-bin.log  # The binary log file location
```

Create a Replication User:

Create a user that the slave server will use to connect to the master server. Replace 'your_user' and 'your_password' with your desired username and password:

```
CREATE USER 'your_user'@'slave_ip' IDENTIFIED BY 'your_password';
GRANT REPLICATION SLAVE ON *.* TO 'your_user'@'slave_ip';
```

Restart MySQL:

Restart the MySQL service to apply the configuration changes:

```
sudo service mysql restart
```

Take a Backup:

Create a consistent backup of the master database using tools like **mysqldump** or a filesystem snapshot to avoid data inconsistencies.

Configure the Slave Server:

On the slave server, perform the following steps:

Configure MySQL Server:

Edit the MySQL configuration file (my.cnf or my.ini) on the slave server. Add the following lines under the **[mysqld]** section:

```
server-id = 2 # A unique server ID for the slave
```

Restore the Backup:

Restore the backup you took from the master server to the slave server. This will ensure the slave starts with the same data as the master.

Start Replication:

Connect to the MySQL server on the slave and issue the following SQL commands to start replication:

```
CHANGE MASTER TO
MASTER_HOST = 'master_ip',   # Replace with the master server's IP address
MASTER_USER = 'your_user',  # The replication user created on the master
MASTER_PASSWORD = 'your_password',
MASTER_LOG_FILE = 'mysql-bin.000001',  # Use the binary log file from the master
MASTER_LOG_POS = 0;
START SLAVE;
```

Replace 'master_ip', 'your_user', 'your_password' with the appropriate values. You can obtain the binary log file and position from the master by executing **SHOW MASTER STATUS;** on the master server.

Check Replication Status:

Check the replication status on the slave server:

```
SHOW SLAVE STATUS\G;
```

Look for the "Slave_IO_Running" and "Slave_SQL_Running" fields. They should both be "Yes," indicating that replication is running.

Verify and Monitor:

Ensure the slave server stays in sync with the master by monitoring replication status and logs.
Perform periodic backups of the slave server to maintain data redundancy.

Failover and Maintenance:

In the event of a master server failure or planned maintenance, you can promote the slave to become the new master. This process involves reconfiguring other slaves to replicate from the new master.
Setting up master-slave replication in MySQL provides a level of redundancy and read scaling. Keep in mind that data consistency and conflict resolution may require additional considerations in complex setups, and it's crucial to maintain backups and monitor replication health.

9.3 Managing Replication

Managing replication in MySQL involves various tasks, such as monitoring, troubleshooting, failover, and reconfiguration, to ensure the replication process runs smoothly. Below, I'll explain the key aspects of managing replication in MySQL with examples:

Checking Replication Status:

You can regularly check the replication status to ensure that the master and slave servers are synchronized and replication is running smoothly.

On the slave server, run:

SHOW SLAVE STATUS\G;

Example output:

```
Slave_IO_State: Waiting for master to send event
Master_Host: master_server_ip
Master_User: replication_user
Master_Port: 3306
Slave_IO_Running: Yes
Slave_SQL_Running: Yes
...
```

In the output, make sure that "Slave_IO_Running" and "Slave_SQL_Running" are both "Yes." If not, investigate and address any issues.

Troubleshooting Replication Issues:

Replication issues can occur due to various reasons, such as network problems, misconfigurations, or data inconsistencies. The error messages and statuses from **SHOW SLAVE STATUS** can help identify and troubleshoot issues.

If replication is not running, review the error message from **SHOW SLAVE STATUS** and the MySQL error log to identify the problem.

If you encounter duplicate key errors on the slave, you can use **STOP SLAVE** and **SET GLOBAL SQL_SLAVE_SKIP_COUNTER** to skip problematic queries. For example:

Failover and Promoting a Slave:

In case of a master server failure, you can promote a slave to become the new master. This involves reconfiguring other slaves to replicate from the new master. Here's an example of the failover process:

On the slave that you want to promote to the new master, stop replication:

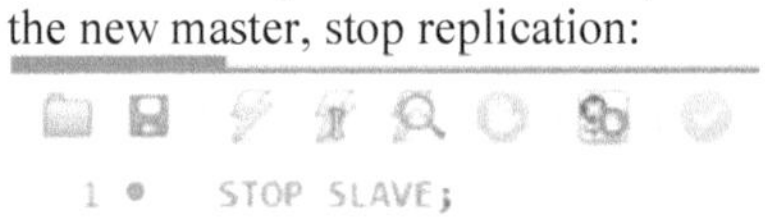

On the application side, reconfigure it to connect to the new master's IP address and port.

If other slaves were replicating from the old master, reconfigure them to replicate from the new master:

```
CHANGE MASTER TO
MASTER_HOST = 'new_master_ip',
MASTER_USER = 'replication_user',
MASTER_PASSWORD = 'replication_password',
MASTER_LOG_FILE = 'new_master_binlog_file',
MASTER_LOG_POS = new_master_binlog_position;
```

Start replication on the new master and other slaves:

Reinitializing a Slave:

In some cases, it may be necessary to reinitialize a slave if data inconsistency or corruption is detected.

On the slave, stop replication:

Clear the data directory:

Create a new consistent backup of the master and restore it on the slave.

Configure replication as if setting up a new slave. Use **CHANGE MASTER TO** to set the replication parameters.

Monitoring Replication Lag:

Replication lag can occur when the slave is behind the master in terms of processing replication events. You can monitor and manage replication lag by checking the timestamps on the master and slave and taking appropriate actions to reduce the lag.

To monitor replication lag, you can run a query on the slave to compare timestamps:

```sql
SELECT NOW() - TIMESTAMP(last_executed) AS replication_lag
FROM information_schema.events_waits_current
WHERE event_name = 'wait/io/file/sql/binlog';
```

To reduce replication lag, consider optimizing queries, increasing server resources, and maintaining an efficient replication infrastructure.

Managing replication in MySQL is an ongoing process that requires regular monitoring and maintenance. Understanding the tools and techniques for troubleshooting, promoting a slave, reinitializing, and monitoring replication lag is essential to ensure the reliability and performance of your MySQL replication setup.

9.4 Failover and Load Balancing

Failover and load balancing are essential components of high availability and scalability in MySQL. They help ensure database availability and distribute database workloads effectively. Here's an explanation of failover and load balancing in MySQL:

Failover in MySQL:

Failover is the process of switching database operations to a backup server when the primary (master) server becomes unavailable due to hardware or software issues. This ensures that applications continue to function even when the primary server experiences downtime. Failover can be manual or automated, depending on the setup.

Components of Failover:

Primary Server: The main MySQL server where the database operations normally take place.

Secondary Server (Backup/Slave): A standby MySQL server that replicates data from the primary server and is ready to take over if the primary server fails.

Load Balancer: A component responsible for routing client requests to the primary server under normal circumstances. In case of a failure, it directs traffic to the secondary server.

How Failover Works:

A monitoring system continuously checks the health of the primary server. If the primary server becomes unresponsive, the monitoring system detects the failure.

When the failure is detected, the load balancer is informed to redirect incoming traffic to the secondary server.

The secondary server takes over as the new primary server, and the database operations continue.

Load Balancing in MySQL:

Load balancing involves distributing incoming database queries across multiple MySQL servers, ensuring even distribution of workload. It helps in achieving better performance and scalability by preventing any single server from becoming a bottleneck.

Components of Load Balancing:

Load Balancer: An intermediary server or software component that receives incoming database queries and routes them to one of the MySQL servers in a cluster. It can be a hardware load balancer or a software-based solution.

MySQL Servers: A group of MySQL servers, often configured in a master-slave or multi-master setup, that process incoming queries.

How Load Balancing Works:

Client applications connect to the load balancer to send their database queries.

The load balancer evaluates the query load on each MySQL server and decides which one to forward the query to.

The selected MySQL server processes the query and sends the response back to the load balancer.

The load balancer forwards the response to the client application.

Combining Failover and Load Balancing:

In many high availability setups, failover and load balancing are combined to create a robust database infrastructure:

Load balancers distribute read queries across multiple MySQL servers to improve read performance.

In case of a primary server failure, the load balancer is reconfigured to route all queries to the secondary server until the primary server is restored.

Automated failover mechanisms ensure minimal downtime by switching to a standby server when the primary server fails.

Example of a Combined Setup:

Two MySQL servers: One as the primary (master) server and the other as the secondary (slave) server.

A load balancer in front of these MySQL servers that routes read queries to the primary server and write queries to the primary server (since write queries typically need to go to the master).

Automated monitoring systems that detect primary server failures and trigger a change in load balancer configuration to direct all traffic to the secondary server until the primary server is restored.

Implementing a combined failover and load balancing setup in MySQL is a common approach for ensuring both high availability and scalability in database systems. It allows for efficient utilization of resources while maintaining database availability.

9.5 Exercise

1. What is the primary goal of high availability in a database system?

a. Minimizing database storage costs

b. Ensuring data consistency and accessibility
c. Maximizing query performance
d. Reducing network latency
2. What is the purpose of database replication in MySQL?
a. Backup and restore
b. Load balancing
c. High availability
d. Data compression
3. In the context of MySQL replication, what is a "Master" server?
a. The server used for development and testing
b. The primary server that handles both reads and writes
c. A server that stores historical data
d. A dedicated backup server
4. In a Master-Slave replication setup, which server(s) allow write operations?
a. Only the Master server
b. Only the Slave server
c. Both Master and Slave servers
d. Neither Master nor Slave servers
5. What is the role of the "Binary Log" in MySQL replication?
a. It stores the database schema.
b. It records all changes made to the Master database.
c. It is a backup of the entire database.
d. It is used for load balancing.
6. Which statement is true about Master-Slave replication lag?
a. It refers to the delay between a write operation on the Master and the update on the Slave.
b. It refers to the delay between two consecutive read operations on the Master.
c. It is always zero and doesn't exist.
d. It only affects the Master server.
7. What is the purpose of a "relay log" in MySQL replication?
a. To store backup data
b. To relay data from the Slave to the Master
c. To store queries for load balancing
d. To archive old data
8. In Master-Slave replication, what happens if the Master server goes down?
a. All read and write operations continue on the Slave server.
b. Both Master and Slave servers go offline.
c. The Slave server takes over as the new Master.
d. Data is lost and cannot be recovered.
9. What is the typical use case for setting up a Master-Slave replication in MySQL?
a. Running analytical queries on the Master server
b. Improving write performance on the Slave server
c. Load balancing read operations across multiple Slaves
d. High availability and disaster recovery
10. Which statement is true about automatic failover in MySQL replication?
a. It requires manual intervention to switch to the Slave server in case of Master failure.
b. It is a built-in feature that automatically promotes a Slave to a Master upon failure.
c. It is not possible in MySQL replication.
d. It requires a third-party tool for implementation.
11. What is the term for ensuring that data changes are applied in the same order on the Slave as on the Master in MySQL replication?
a. Consistency
b. Parallelism
c. Redundancy
d. Isolation
12. In MySQL replication, what is the purpose of the "CHANGE MASTER TO" statement?
a. To change the database schema on the Slave server.
b. To modify the data on the Master server.
c. To configure the Slave to replicate from a different Master.
d. To encrypt data during replication.

13. Which replication mode in MySQL provides asynchronous replication without guaranteeing that data is consistent between Master and Slave?
a. Synchronous replication
b. Semi-synchronous replication
c. Asynchronous replication
d. Real-time replication
14. In a Master-Slave replication setup, what is the process called when a Slave requests data changes from the Master?
a. Mirroring
b. Cloning
c. Binlog retrieval
d. Replication synchronization
15. Which of the following statements are true regarding high availability and Master-Slave replication in MySQL?
a. Master-Slave replication provides automatic failover.
b. High availability aims to minimize downtime and data loss.
c. Replication lag refers to the delay between a write operation on the Slave and the update on the Master.
d. Automatic failover can be achieved using third-party tools.
16. What is database replication in MySQL?
a. Storing multiple copies of the same data for redundancy
b. Mirroring the entire database structure in a single instance
c. Backing up the database periodically
d. Splitting a database into multiple smaller databases
17. What is the primary purpose of database replication in MySQL?
a. To eliminate the need for backups
b. To distribute read and write operations across multiple database servers
c. To improve data security
d. To reduce the number of database users
18. In MySQL replication, what is the role of the "master" server?
a. It is responsible for handling read queries.
b. It is responsible for distributing write queries.
c. It stores a copy of the data from the "slave" servers.
d. It manages the failover process.
19. What is a "slave" server in MySQL replication?
a. A server that replicates data from the "master" server.
b. A server that controls the write operations.
c. A server that stores backup copies of the data.
d. A server that handles all database queries.
20. In MySQL replication, what is binlog (binary log)?
a. A database table used to store binary data.
b. A type of log that contains a record of changes to the database.
c. A binary representation of the entire database.
d. A tool used for load balancing.
21. What is the purpose of MySQL failover?
a. To create redundant copies of data for read operations.
b. To eliminate the need for backups.
c. To ensure high availability by automatically switching to a standby server in case of a failure.
d. To distribute write operations across multiple servers.
22. Which type of failover mechanism in MySQL automatically promotes a standby server to the master role if the current master fails?
a. Manual failover
b. Automatic failover
c. Semi-synchronous replication
d. Parallel replication
23. What is a "read replica" in MySQL?
a. A server that handles write operations.
b. A backup server.
c. A server that replicates data from the master for read operations.
d. A server that stores historical data.
24. How can you achieve load balancing in MySQL?
a. By configuring the "master" server to handle all database queries.

b. By configuring multiple "slave" servers to distribute write operations.
c. By using a load balancer to distribute database queries across multiple database servers.
d. By creating redundant copies of the database for high availability.
25. Which of the following is an example of a MySQL load balancing tool or technology?
a. MySQL Router
b. MySQL Workbench
c. MySQL Cluster
d. MySQL Shell
26. In MySQL, what is the purpose of GTID (Global Transaction ID)?
a. To store encrypted data.
b. To identify unique transactions in a replication setup.
c. To synchronize the system time between multiple database servers.
d. To perform automatic failover.
27. Which of the following is a common method for load balancing read operations in MySQL?
a. Using a reverse proxy server
b. Replicating the entire database
c. Creating a single, centralized database server
d. Manually dividing read queries between servers
28. In MySQL replication, what is "semi-synchronous replication"?
a. A mode where only half of the data is replicated.
b. A type of replication where transactions are acknowledged by at least one slave before they are committed on the master.
c. Replicating data only from the master server to the slave server.
d. A mechanism to prevent replication altogether.
29. Which of the following is NOT a benefit of MySQL replication?
a. Improved data security
b. Load balancing for read operations
c. High availability and failover capabilities
d. Elimination of the need for backups
30. What is the primary use case for MySQL replication?
a. Improving data integrity
b. Reducing the number of database users
c. Scaling out read operations and achieving high availability
d. Simplifying the database schema.

Answer

1) b. 2) c. 3) b. 4) a. 5) b. 6) a. 7) b. 8) b. 9) d. 10) d. 11) a. 12) c. 13) c. 14) d. 15) b, d. 16) a. 17) b. 18) b. 19) a. 20) b. 21) c. 22) b. 23) c. 24) c. 25) a. 26) b. 27) a. 28) b. 29) d. 30) c.

ONLINE RESOURCES

Practice Paper
Link: https://forms.gle/bEyB2v2JXyZhnRcJ7
QR Code:

Video Content:
Link: https://www.youtube.com/playlist?list=PLzlh_31VWEFqEaja4Jqbe3YFLxNAPMMe4
QR Code:

10.1 Authentication Methods

MySQL provides several authentication methods to ensure the security of your database. These methods help control who can access the MySQL server and what actions they can perform. Here are some of the commonly used authentication methods in MySQL security:

Native MySQL Authentication:

Username/Password: The traditional username and password combination is the default and most common authentication method. Users must provide valid credentials to access the MySQL server.

Example:

```
CREATE USER 'username'@'localhost' IDENTIFIED BY 'password';
```

Pluggable Authentication:

MySQL introduced pluggable authentication in MySQL 5.7. It allows users to choose from various authentication plugins or develop custom plugins. Some common authentication plugins are:

caching_sha2_password: This is the default authentication plugin in MySQL 8.0. It supports improved security features like SHA-256 password hashing.

Example:

```
CREATE USER 'username'@'localhost' IDENTIFIED WITH 'caching_sha2_password' BY 'password';
```

mysql_native_password: This is the traditional MySQL password hashing method.

Example:

```
CREATE USER 'username'@'localhost' IDENTIFIED WITH 'mysql_native_password' BY 'password';
```

unix_socket: With this method, authentication is based on the user's operating system user account rather than a password. This is common for local connections.

Example:

```
CREATE USER 'username'@'localhost' IDENTIFIED VIA unix_socket;
```

External Authentication:

MySQL allows integration with external authentication methods, such as LDAP, PAM, or Windows Active Directory. This enables centralized user management and authentication.

LDAP: MySQL can authenticate users against an LDAP server. It's commonly used in enterprise environments for centralized user management.

Example:

```
CREATE USER 'username'@'localhost' IDENTIFIED WITH 'authentication_ldap';
```

PAM (Pluggable Authentication Module): PAM integration allows MySQL to use system-level authentication methods configured through PAM.

Example:

```
CREATE USER 'username'@'localhost' IDENTIFIED WITH 'authentication_pam';
```

SSL/TLS Authentication:

MySQL supports secure connections using SSL/TLS protocols. This method is often used for securing data in transit and for authenticating clients with SSL certificates.

X.509 Certificates: Users can be authenticated based on X.509 digital certificates. You can configure MySQL to require SSL connections and verify client certificates.

Example (configuring MySQL for SSL):

```
[mysqld]
ssl-ca=/etc/mysql/ssl/ca.pem
ssl-cert=/etc/mysql/ssl/server-cert.pem
ssl-key=/etc/mysql/ssl/server-key.pem
require_secure_transport=ON
```

OAuth 2.0 Authentication:
Starting with MySQL 8.0.14, you can use OAuth 2.0 for authentication. Users authenticate using OAuth 2.0 tokens obtained from an identity provider like Google.
OAuth 2.0: This method is useful for cloud-based authentication where users authenticate with their Google accounts.

Example:

```sql
CREATE USER 'username'@'localhost' IDENTIFIED WITH 'authentication_oauth';
```

Two-Factor Authentication (2FA):
MySQL can be configured to require two-factor authentication for user logins. This adds an additional layer of security by combining a password with a secondary authentication factor, such as a one-time code from a mobile app.
2FA: Some MySQL clients and authentication plugins support two-factor authentication for enhanced security.

These are some of the authentication methods you can use in MySQL to secure your database. The choice of method depends on your security requirements, user management policies, and application architecture. It's essential to use strong authentication methods and regularly review and update your security practices to protect your MySQL database effectively.

10.2 Authorization and Permissions

Authorization and permissions in MySQL are fundamental aspects of database security. They control who can access the database, what actions they can perform, and on which database objects (such as tables, views, and procedures) they can operate. Here's a comprehensive explanation of authorization and permissions in MySQL security:

User Accounts:

Creating User Accounts:

User accounts are at the core of MySQL's security model. To create a user account, use the **CREATE USER** statement:

```sql
CREATE USER 'username'@'localhost' IDENTIFIED BY 'password';
```

The **'username'** is the username for the account, **'localhost'** specifies where the user can connect from, and **'password'** is the user's password.

Privileges and Permissions:
MySQL provides a comprehensive system of privileges and permissions that specify what users can do in the database. Privileges encompass actions like SELECT, INSERT, UPDATE, DELETE, CREATE, DROP, and more.

Granting Privileges:

To grant privileges to a user, use the **GRANT** statement:

```sql
GRANT SELECT, INSERT ON database_name.* TO 'username'@'localhost';
```

This statement grants the user the privilege to SELECT and INSERT data in all tables within the specified database.

Revoking Privileges:

To revoke privileges from a user, use the **REVOKE** statement:

```sql
REVOKE INSERT ON database_name.* FROM 'username'@'localhost';
```

Privilege Levels:
MySQL supports various privilege levels, allowing you to control access at different levels of granularity:

Global Privileges:

These apply to the entire MySQL server and all its databases.

Database Privileges:

These apply to specific databases.

Table Privileges:

These control access to specific tables within a database.

Column Privileges:

You can also grant or revoke privileges on individual columns within a table.

Roles:
Roles are collections of privileges and are used to simplify the management of user permissions. You can grant roles to users, reducing the need to manage individual privileges.

Creating Roles:

To create a role, use the **CREATE ROLE** statement:

```sql
CREATE ROLE 'role_name';
```

Assigning Roles:

You can assign roles to users using the **GRANT** statement as well:

Checking User Privileges:

You can check the privileges assigned to a user using the **SHOW GRANTS** statement:

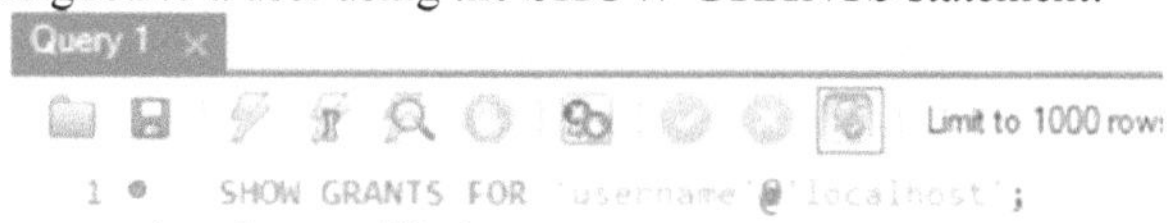

This will display the privileges granted to the specified user.

Security Best Practices:

Principle of Least Privilege: Follow the principle of least privilege, granting only the minimum necessary privileges to users and roles to perform their tasks.

Strong Passwords: Encourage users to use strong, complex passwords.

Regular Review: Periodically review and audit user accounts and permissions to ensure alignment with security policies.

SSL/TLS Encryption: Use SSL/TLS encryption for secure client-server communication.

Limit Remote Access: Limit exposure to the internet and use firewall rules to restrict remote access.

Audit Logs: Enable and monitor MySQL's audit logs to track user activity.

Prevent SQL Injection: Utilize prepared statements, stored procedures, and input validation to prevent SQL injection attacks.

Database Views: Use views to control what data users can see.

MySQL's authorization and permissions system provide a powerful means of securing your database. Properly configuring and managing these permissions is crucial to maintaining the security and integrity of your MySQL database.

10.3 Best Practices for Security

Securing a MySQL database is critical to protect your data and ensure the reliability of your applications. Here are some best practices for enhancing security in MySQL:

Regularly Update MySQL:

Ensure you are using the latest version of MySQL and keep it updated with security patches and bug fixes.

Strong Authentication:

Use strong, complex passwords for user accounts.

Enforce password policies, such as password length and complexity requirements.

Avoid using default usernames like "root" or "admin" for database administration.

Least Privilege Principle:

Follow the principle of least privilege, which means granting users and applications only the minimum privileges they need to perform their tasks. Avoid giving unnecessary global or administrative privileges.

Secure Network Access:

Limit exposure to the internet. Use a firewall to control access to your MySQL server.

Consider using a Virtual Private Cloud (VPC) or network-level security groups to isolate your MySQL server from unauthorized access.

Enable SSL/TLS encryption for secure client-server communication.

Database User Accounts:

Create separate user accounts for different applications or components of your system.

Avoid using root or superuser accounts for application connections.

Restrict user access based on the principle of least privilege.

Monitor User Activity:

Use MySQL's audit logs to track user activity, including login attempts, SQL queries, and modifications to privileges.

Monitor for unusual or suspicious behavior.

Backup and Recovery:

Regularly back up your data and test your backups to ensure they are working correctly.

Implement a disaster recovery plan for quick recovery in case of data loss.

Input Validation:

Always validate and sanitize user inputs to prevent SQL injection attacks.

Use parameterized queries and prepared statements in your application code.

Prevent Cross-Site Scripting (XSS):

Implement security measures to prevent cross-site scripting attacks in your web applications.

Avoid embedding user inputs directly into HTML, JavaScript, or other code without proper encoding.

Secure SQL Queries:

Avoid dynamic SQL queries built from user inputs whenever possible.

Sanitize and validate user inputs to prevent SQL injection vulnerabilities.

Limit File Permissions:

Restrict file permissions on the server hosting the MySQL server to prevent unauthorized access.

Use file system access controls and encryption for sensitive data files.

Disable Unnecessary Features:
Disable or restrict access to MySQL features and functionality that are not needed for your specific use case.
Remove or disable unnecessary plugins and components.
Regularly Review and Audit:
Periodically review user accounts and permissions to ensure they align with your organization's security policies.
Conduct security audits to identify vulnerabilities.
Use Web Application Firewalls (WAFs):
Implement web application firewalls to filter and block malicious traffic before it reaches your application and database.
Implement Role-Based Access Control:
Use roles to simplify permission management. Assign roles to users to group common privileges.
Regularly review and update role assignments as your application's requirements change.
Two-Factor Authentication (2FA):
Implement 2FA for database administrators and other privileged users to enhance security.
Secure Stored Procedures:
Use stored procedures to prevent SQL injection and manage database operations.
Avoid dynamic SQL in stored procedures whenever possible.
Regularly Test Security:
Conduct security testing, including vulnerability assessments and penetration testing.
Implement security testing as part of the development lifecycle.
Keep Application and Frameworks Updated:
Ensure that your application code and web frameworks are up to date with security patches and updates.
Stay Informed:
Stay informed about the latest security threats, vulnerabilities, and best practices. Subscribe to security bulletins and updates from MySQL and security organizations.

Security is an ongoing process. Regularly review and update your security measures to adapt to evolving threats and ensure the safety of your MySQL database and sensitive data.

10.4 Data Encryption and Auditing

Data encryption and auditing are essential components of MySQL security. Encryption helps protect data at rest and in transit, while auditing enables you to monitor and track database activities. Here's a detailed explanation of data encryption and auditing in MySQL security:
Data Encryption in MySQL:
Data at Rest Encryption:

MySQL supports data-at-rest encryption to protect your data stored on disk. This can be achieved using technologies like Transparent Data Encryption (TDE) or full-disk encryption. TDE encrypts the entire database or specific tables.
To enable TDE in MySQL, you can use third-party encryption tools or solutions, as MySQL does not natively provide TDE.
Third-party solutions like Oracle MySQL Enterprise Transparent Data Encryption can provide this functionality.

Data in Transit Encryption:

MySQL supports secure data transmission through SSL/TLS. Enabling SSL/TLS ensures that data sent between the client and the server is encrypted.
To enable SSL/TLS encryption, you need to configure MySQL to use SSL certificates and update your client applications to connect using a secure connection.
Example configuration in the MySQL server's my.cnf or my.ini file:

```
[mysqld]
ssl-ca=/etc/mysql/ssl/ca.pem
ssl-cert=/etc/mysql/ssl/server-cert.pem
ssl-key=/etc/mysql/ssl/server-key.pem
require_secure_transport=ON
```

Client-Side Encryption:

For end-to-end encryption, you can implement client-side encryption. This involves encrypting data on the client side before it's sent to the database and decrypting it on retrieval.
Client-side encryption can be achieved through application-level encryption libraries or encryption middleware.

Auditing in MySQL:
MySQL Enterprise Audit Plugin:

MySQL offers the Enterprise Audit Plugin, which enables comprehensive auditing capabilities.
The audit plugin can record a wide range of events, including logins, queries, DDL statements, and data modifications.
It supports various output destinations, including files, tables, and the system log.
Example installation and configuration:

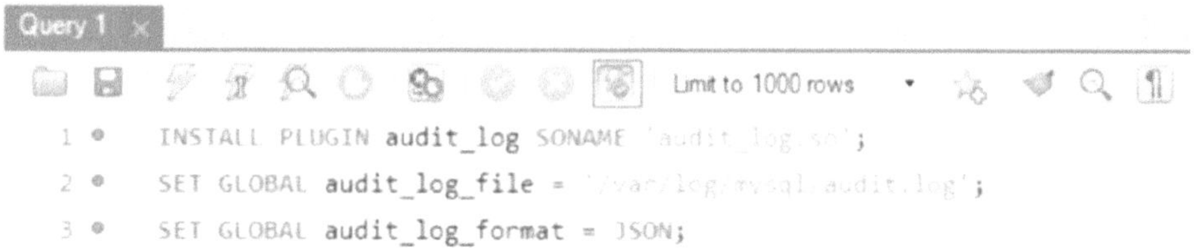

General Query Log and Slow Query Log:

MySQL also provides general query and slow query logs, which can be configured to record specific types of activities.

The general query log records all queries executed on the server, which can be helpful for debugging and auditing.

The slow query log records queries that exceed a specified execution time, helping identify performance bottlenecks.

Example configuration:

```
[mysqld]
general_log = 1
general_log_file = /var/log/mysql/general.log
slow_query_log = 1
slow_query_log_file = /var/log/mysql/slow-query.log
long_query_time = 1
```

Third-Party Auditing Tools:

Numerous third-party tools and services provide advanced auditing and monitoring capabilities for MySQL databases. Some popular options include Imperva SecureSphere, McAfee Database Security, and IBM Guardium.

Custom Auditing Solutions:

You can build custom auditing solutions by implementing triggers, stored procedures, and application-level auditing mechanisms. These methods allow you to record specific database events tailored to your application's requirements.

Best Practices:

Enable SSL/TLS encryption to secure data in transit.
Use third-party solutions for data-at-rest encryption if needed.
Implement comprehensive auditing with the MySQL Enterprise Audit Plugin or use the general query and slow query logs.
Store audit logs in a secure location with limited access.
Regularly review audit logs to detect unusual or unauthorized activities.
Ensure that client-side applications handle encryption and decryption securely.
Keep MySQL and auditing solutions up to date with the latest security patches and updates.
By implementing data encryption and auditing in MySQL, you can enhance the security and compliance of your database system, protecting sensitive data and monitoring database activities for potential security threats.

10.5 Exercise

1. Which authentication method in MySQL involves checking the client's IP address against a list of allowed hosts?
a. Password-based authentication
b. IP-based authentication
c. SSL-based authentication
d. LDAP-based authentication
2. In MySQL, what is the purpose of the authentication plugin "caching_sha2_password"?
a. Encrypt user passwords
b. Store and manage SSL certificates
c. Cache query results for faster access
d. Authenticate users securely
3. What authentication method is used when connecting to MySQL over a secure SSL/TLS connection?
a. PAM-based authentication
b. X.509 authentication
c. SHA-256 authentication
d. OAuth-based authentication
4. Which authentication method is used to integrate MySQL with an external directory service such as Microsoft Active Directory?
a. PAM-based authentication
b. X.509 authentication
c. OAuth-based authentication
d. LDAP-based authentication
5. What minimum privilege level is required to execute the "SELECT" statement in MySQL?

a. SUPER
b. SELECT
c. INSERT
d. USAGE
6. In MySQL, what privilege allows a user to create and modify databases and tables?
a. SELECT
b. DROP
c. CREATE
d. UPDATE
7. Which statement is true regarding MySQL user accounts?
a. A user account is tied to a single host.
b. A user account can be used from any host without restriction.
c. A user account can have different privileges on different hosts.
d. User accounts are global and not host-specific.
8. What MySQL privilege is required to grant privileges to other users?
a. SUPER
b. GRANT OPTION
c. CREATE USER
d. SELECT
9. What is a recommended best practice for securing MySQL?
a. Use easily guessable passwords.
b. Grant all privileges to all users.
c. Regularly update and patch MySQL.
d. Allow anonymous user access.
10. What is the purpose of regularly reviewing and revoking unnecessary privileges in MySQL?
a. To improve performance
b. To simplify user account management
c. To reduce security risks
d. To increase database size
11. Which of the following is a best practice for securing MySQL data?
a. Store sensitive data in plain text.
b. Use SSL for encrypting data in transit.
c. Share database credentials with colleagues.
d. Use weak passwords.
12. What is the primary purpose of data encryption in MySQL?
a. To improve query performance
b. To secure data at rest and in transit
c. To restrict user access
d. To create data backups
13. Which encryption type is used to secure data at rest in MySQL?
a. SSL
b. AES
c. RSA
d. SHA-256
14. What does the MySQL query "SHOW VARIABLES LIKE 'general_log';" display information about?
a. Database structure
b. General server settings
c. Query logging
d. User privileges
15. What is the purpose of the MySQL General Query Log?
a. It records all changes to the database.
b. It logs user authentication events.
c. It records all SQL statements executed on the server.
d. It monitors CPU and memory usage.
16. What is the purpose of managing users and privileges in MySQL?
a. To optimize database performance
b. To enhance data security and control access
c. To update the MySQL software
d. To perform backups

17. Which privilege is required for creating new users in MySQL?
a. SELECT
b. INSERT
c. CREATE USER
d. DROP USER
18. In MySQL, what is the "root" user?
a. The user with the highest privilege
b. A regular user with limited access
c. A reserved username for backups
d. A user with read-only access
19. Which SQL statement is used to grant specific privileges to a user in MySQL?
a. GRANT
b. CREATE USER
c. INSERT
d. REVOKE
20. What does the "ALL PRIVILEGES" keyword represent when granting privileges in MySQL?
a. It grants all available privileges on all databases.
b. It grants the SELECT privilege only.
c. It grants read-only access.
d. It revokes all existing privileges.
21. In MySQL, what is the purpose of the "FLUSH PRIVILEGES" command?
a. To exit the MySQL server
b. To start a new transaction
c. To reload the grant tables and apply privilege changes
d. To change a user's password
22. What is the default authentication method for MySQL users?
a. Passwordless authentication
b. LDAP authentication
c. SHA-256 password hashing
d. Native password authentication
23. How can you change a user's password in MySQL?
a. Using the ALTER USER statement
b. Using the DELETE USER statement
c. Using the SET PASSWORD statement
d. Using the GRANT statement
24. When removing a user in MySQL, what privilege is required?
a. DELETE USER
b. DROP USER
c. REVOKE
d. SELECT
25. What happens when you use the "DROP USER" statement in MySQL to remove a user?
a. The user is permanently deleted, and all data is lost.
b. The user is suspended temporarily.
c. The user's privileges are revoked, but the user account remains.
d. The user is renamed to "anonymous."
26. What is the purpose of the "WITH GRANT OPTION" when granting privileges in MySQL?
a. It allows the user to create new users.
b. It allows the user to revoke their own privileges.
c. It is not a valid option in MySQL.
d. It grants all available privileges.
27. Which statement is used to display the list of MySQL users?
a. SHOW DATABASES;
b. SHOW USERS;
c. SHOW PRIVILEGES;
d. SELECT USER();
28. What privilege is required to change the password of another user in MySQL?
a. ALTER USER
b. CHANGE PASSWORD
c. UPDATE

d. SUPER
29. In MySQL, what is the purpose of the "REVOKE" statement?
a. To grant privileges to a user
b. To change a user's password
c. To remove specific privileges from a user
d. To add a new user
30. What happens when a user's privileges are revoked in MySQL?
a. The user account is deleted.
b. The user account remains, but they lose the specified privileges.
c. The user's password is reset.
d. The user is granted additional privileges.

Answer

1) b. 2) d. 3) b. 4) d. 5) b. 6) c. 7) c. 8) b. 9) c. 10) d. 11) b. 12) b. 13) b. 14) c. 15) c. 16) b. 17) c. 18) a. 19) a. 20) a. 21) c. 22) d. 23) c. 24) b. 25) a. 26) a. 27) d. 28) a. 29) c. 30) b.

ONLINE RESOURCES

Practice Paper
Link: https://forms.gle/QZVgwpbBkRUyjHDX7
QR Code:

Video Content:
Link: https://www.youtube.com/playlist?list=PLzlh_31VWEFqBCnbj1-XKKcftPVRZ8UAO
QR Code:

Chapter 11: Advanced Topics

11.1 Full-Text Search

Full-Text Search in MySQL is a powerful feature that allows you to perform text-based searches on text and character-based data stored in your database. It is particularly useful for applications like content management systems, e-commerce platforms, and forums where users need to search for specific words or phrases within large volumes of text. Here's an overview of Full-Text Search in MySQL:

Creating a Full-Text Index:

To perform Full-Text Searches, you need to create a Full-Text Index on the columns you want to search within. You can create a Full-Text Index on one or more columns of a table.

Example of creating a Full-Text Index on a 'content' column in a table named 'articles':

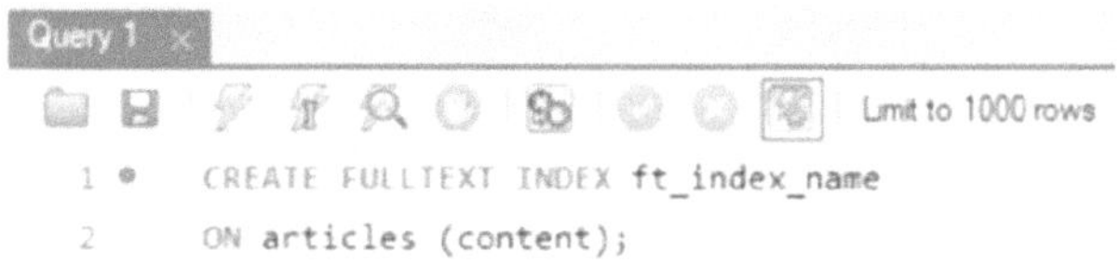

Running Full-Text Searches:

Once you have created a Full-Text Index, you can use the **MATCH()** and **AGAINST()** clauses to run Full-Text Searches. Here's how to perform a basic Full-Text Search:

MATCH() specifies the columns you want to search within (e.g., **content**).

AGAINST() is used to specify the search query.

Boolean Mode:

MySQL's Full-Text Search supports Boolean mode, which allows you to perform more complex searches. You can use operators like +, -, and *, as well as quotation marks to specify exact phrases.

Example using Boolean mode for a Full-Text Search:

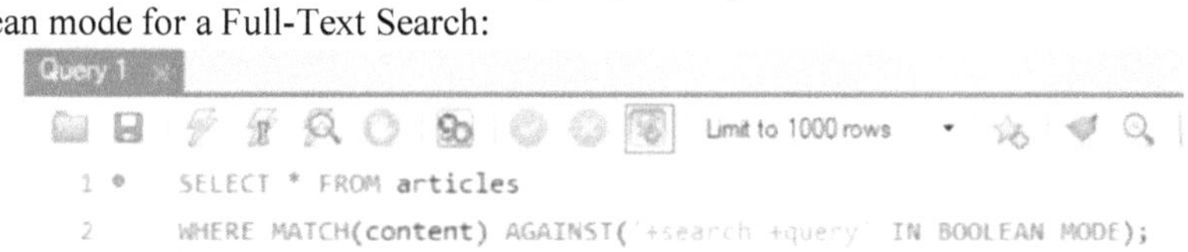

Natural Language Mode:

In Natural Language mode (the default), MySQL assigns different weights to words in the search query and ranks the results accordingly. This is useful for finding relevant results based on the relevance of the search terms.

Example using Natural Language mode for a Full-Text Search:

Minimum Word Length:

By default, MySQL's Full-Text Search excludes words that are too short (usually less than four characters). You can configure the minimum word length using the **ft_min_word_len** system variable.

Stopwords:

Stopwords are common words like "and," "the," "is," and "it," which are ignored in Full-Text Searches by default. You can customize the list of stopwords using the **ft_stopword_file** system variable.

Thesaurus Support:

MySQL provides the ability to define synonyms for words using a thesaurus file. You can configure the thesaurus file using the **ft_thesaurus_file** system variable.

Performance Considerations:

Full-Text Searches can be resource-intensive, especially on large datasets. To improve performance, consider using an appropriate storage engine, optimizing queries, and caching search results.

Advanced Features:

MySQL's Full-Text Search also supports advanced features like the **IN BOOLEAN MODE** modifier, boolean operators, and natural language mode. These features allow you to fine-tune your searches for specific requirements.

Full-Text Search in MySQL is a valuable feature for applications that require efficient text-based searches. Whether you're building a search engine, a content management system, or an e-commerce platform, understanding and utilizing Full-Text Search can greatly enhance the user experience and the functionality of your application.

11.2 Spatial Data and GIS

Spatial data and Geographic Information Systems (GIS) support in MySQL allow you to store, manage, and query geographic and geometric data. This is particularly useful for applications that deal with location-based information, such as mapping, navigation, and spatial analysis. Here's an overview of spatial data and GIS in MySQL:

Spatial Data Types:

MySQL supports several spatial data types for representing geographic and geometric data:

POINT: Represents a single geographic point.

LINESTRING: Represents a sequence of points, forming a line.

POLYGON: Represents a closed ring of points, forming a polygon.

MULTIPOINT: Represents a collection of points.

MULTILINESTRING: Represents a collection of linestrings.

MULTIPOLYGON: Represents a collection of polygons.

GEOMETRY: A generic spatial data type that can represent any of the above types.

Spatial Functions:

MySQL provides a set of spatial functions to manipulate and analyze spatial data. Some common spatial functions include:

ST_DISTANCE: Calculates the distance between two spatial objects.

ST_AREA: Computes the area of a polygon.

ST_LENGTH: Calculates the length of a linestring.

ST_INTERSECTS: Determines whether two spatial objects intersect.

ST_WITHIN: Checks if one object is completely inside another.

Indexing and Optimization:

To improve the performance of spatial queries, MySQL supports spatial indexing using the **SPATIAL** keyword when creating indexes. Spatial indexes help speed up queries that involve spatial data by organizing and optimizing the data for quick retrieval.

GIS Functions:

MySQL supports the use of GIS functions and extensions, making it compatible with many GIS libraries and tools. You can work with GIS data and use MySQL as a backend for GIS applications.

Geometry Data Import and Export:

You can import and export spatial data in various formats, such as Well-Known Text (WKT) and Keyhole Markup Language (KML). This is useful for interoperability with other GIS systems and tools.

Use Cases for Spatial Data:

Mapping Applications: Spatial data in MySQL is ideal for creating maps, geolocation services, and navigation applications.

Geospatial Analysis: Spatial data can be used for geospatial analysis, such as determining the distance between two points, finding the nearest location, or analyzing spatial relationships.

Geofencing: You can create geofences for tracking and notifications when objects enter or leave specific geographic areas.

Environmental Monitoring: Spatial data can be used in environmental monitoring and resource management.

Urban Planning: Urban planners can use spatial data for city planning and development projects.

Geographic Information Systems (GIS):

MySQL can be integrated with full-fledged GIS software and tools, such as QGIS, ArcGIS, or MapServer. These tools can leverage MySQL as a database backend for storing and querying spatial data.

Data Sources:

You can collect spatial data from various sources, including GPS devices, sensors, geospatial surveys, and remote sensing technologies. This data can be stored and analyzed in MySQL.

Security and Permissions:

Ensure that you have appropriate security measures in place to protect your spatial data, as it can contain sensitive location-based information.

Compatibility:

MySQL's spatial data support is compatible with the Open Geospatial Consortium (OGC) standards, making it interoperable with other GIS systems.

MySQL's support for spatial data and GIS features makes it a versatile database system for applications that require geographic and geometric data analysis. Whether you're building location-based services, conducting spatial analysis, or managing geographical data, MySQL's spatial data capabilities can play a crucial role in your application's success.

11.3 JSON Data in MySQL

Storing and querying JSON data in MySQL is a powerful feature that allows you to work with semi-structured and flexible data. JSON, or JavaScript Object Notation, is a widely used data interchange format that is commonly used for data storage and exchange between applications. MySQL has introduced support for JSON data types and functions to work with JSON data efficiently. Here's an overview of working with JSON data in MySQL:

JSON Data Types:

MySQL supports two JSON data types:

JSON: This data type stores JSON data in a compact binary format. It is suitable for storing JSON documents when exact character storage is not required.

JSON (Text): This data type stores JSON data as a text string in a JSON format. It is more human-readable but takes up more space compared to the binary JSON type.

Storing JSON Data:

To store JSON data in a MySQL table, you need to use one of the JSON data types. For example:

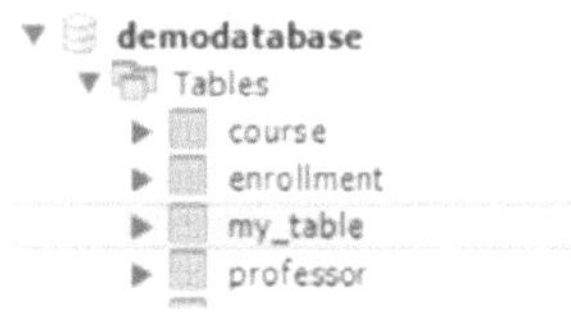

You can insert JSON data into the table as follows:

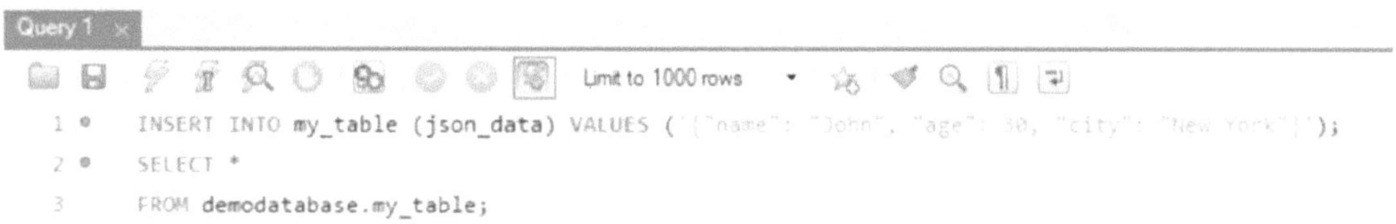

Output:

Querying JSON Data:

MySQL provides a set of JSON functions and operators that allow you to query, extract, and manipulate JSON data within the database. Some common JSON functions include:

JSON_EXTRACT(): Used to extract data from a JSON document.

JSON_SET(): Modifies a JSON document by adding or updating values.

JSON_REMOVE(): Removes elements from a JSON document.

JSON_SEARCH(): Searches for a specified value in a JSON document.

Indexing JSON Data:

To improve the performance of JSON queries, you can create indexes on JSON columns. MySQL allows indexing on JSON attributes for faster retrieval.

Aggregating JSON Data:

MySQL supports aggregation functions for JSON data, such as JSON_ARRAYAGG(), which aggregates values into a JSON array, and JSON_OBJECTAGG(), which creates a JSON object from key-value pairs.

Validating JSON Data:

You can validate JSON data using the JSON_VALID() function to check if it conforms to the JSON format.

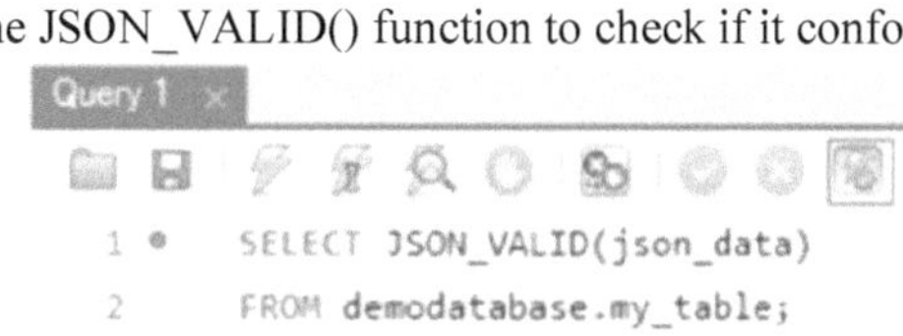

Filtering JSON Data:

You can filter rows based on JSON content by using JSON functions in the WHERE clause of your queries. For example:

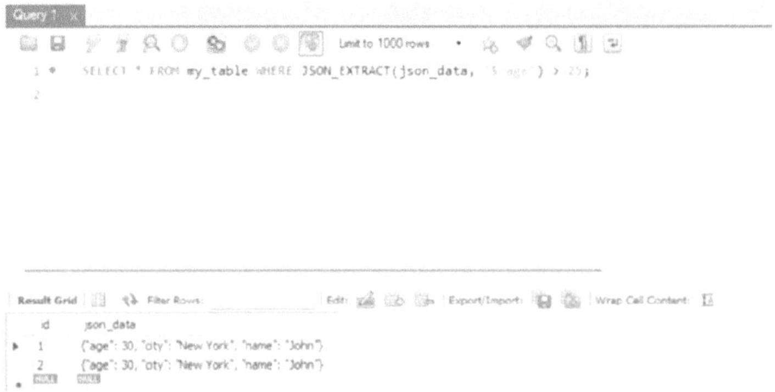

Creating JSON Documents:

You can create JSON documents using MySQL's JSON functions to build structured JSON data within your queries.

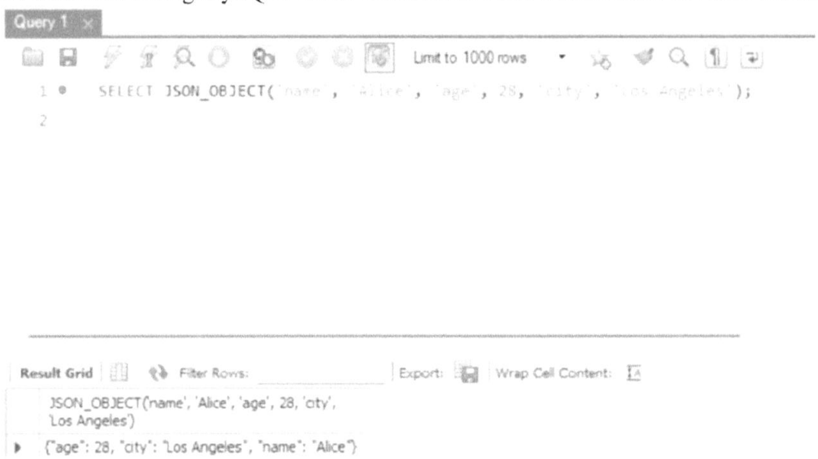

Joins and JSON Data:

You can perform joins between tables that include JSON data and use JSON functions to join and filter data based on JSON attributes.

Security and Validation:

When working with JSON data from untrusted sources, it's essential to validate and sanitize the input to prevent potential security vulnerabilities like SQL injection.

JSON support in MySQL is a versatile feature that allows you to work with semi-structured data efficiently. It is particularly valuable for applications that need to store, query, and manipulate JSON data. Whether you're building web applications, handling API responses, or managing configuration data, MySQL's JSON capabilities offer flexibility and power for working with JSON data.

11.4 Using NoSQL Features

MySQL, primarily known as a relational database management system (RDBMS), has evolved over the years to incorporate some NoSQL features. While it may not be a pure NoSQL database, MySQL offers several capabilities that are reminiscent of NoSQL databases, allowing you to work with semi-structured and unstructured data in a more flexible manner. Here are some NoSQL features and concepts that can be used in MySQL:

JSON Data Type and Functions:

MySQL introduced JSON support, allowing you to store, query, and manipulate JSON data. You can use the JSON data type to store JSON documents and leverage JSON functions to work with this semi-structured data, making MySQL more flexible in handling unstructured or rapidly changing data.

Flexible Schema:

Unlike traditional relational databases, MySQL allows you to have flexible schema designs. You can add or modify columns, which is similar to the way NoSQL databases adapt to changing data requirements.

Key-Value Stores:

You can use MySQL as a key-value store by creating tables with simple key-value structures. This approach is often suitable for caching or storing configuration data.

Document Stores:

MySQL can serve as a document store by utilizing the JSON data type. You can store JSON documents within rows and query them in a NoSQL-like fashion.

NoSQL Connector/Driver:

MySQL provides NoSQL connectors/drivers for various programming languages (e.g., MySQL Connector/Node.js) that allow you to interact with MySQL as a NoSQL database, using JavaScript-like APIs for JSON operations.

High Availability and Scalability:

MySQL can be configured for high availability and horizontal scalability using technologies like MySQL Group Replication and MySQL Router. These features make it more suitable for handling large and distributed data, similar to NoSQL databases.

Caching with Memcached:

MySQL has integration with Memcached, a distributed memory caching system. This combination can be used to accelerate read-heavy workloads by caching frequently accessed data.

Spatial Data and GIS:

MySQL's support for spatial data and GIS features allows you to work with geospatial and location-based data, making it suitable for applications that require NoSQL-like handling of geographic data.

Full-Text Search:

MySQL provides Full-Text Search capabilities that can be useful for text-based searches in unstructured data, such as documents or content from websites.

Data Sharding:

MySQL supports data sharding techniques, which are commonly used in NoSQL databases to distribute data across multiple servers or clusters for scalability and performance.

Multi-Version Concurrency Control (MVCC):

MySQL uses MVCC to handle concurrent access to data, allowing multiple users to read and write data without locking the entire table. This is a feature shared with many NoSQL databases.

In-Memory Storage Engine:

MySQL offers the InnoDB Memcached plugin, which allows data to be stored and retrieved directly from memory, offering fast data access similar to in-memory NoSQL databases.

While MySQL offers some NoSQL-like features, it's essential to recognize that it remains a relational database at its core. These NoSQL features provide flexibility for specific use cases, but MySQL's strengths still lie in the relational model. When considering using NoSQL features in MySQL, carefully assess your application's requirements and determine whether MySQL's capabilities align with your data model and scalability needs.

11.5 Exercise

1. What is Full-Text Search in MySQL primarily used for?

a. Searching for exact matches in a table
b. Performing case-sensitive searches
c. Finding partial and approximate matches in text data
d. Indexing numeric data

2. Which storage engine in MySQL is commonly used for Full-Text Search?

a. InnoDB
b. MyISAM
c. MEMORY
d. NDB

3. In a Full-Text Search query, which operator is used to search for documents containing multiple keywords?

a. AND
b. OR
c. NOT
d. XOR

4. Which MySQL statement is used to create a Full-Text Search index on a table?

a. CREATE TABLE
b. CREATE INDEX
c. CREATE FULLTEXT INDEX
d. CREATE SEARCH INDEX

5. When using Full-Text Search, which MySQL function is commonly used to rank the relevance of search results?

a. RANK()
b. SCORE()
c. MATCH()
d. CONTAINS()

6. What does the asterisk (*) character represent in a Full-Text Search query in MySQL?

a. A wildcard character for any single character
b. A wildcard character for zero or more characters
c. A literal asterisk character
d. A placeholder for a numeric value

7. Which modifier can be used to perform a case-insensitive Full-Text Search in MySQL?

a. CASESENSITIVE
b. COLLATE
c. IGNORECASE
d. CASEINSENSITIVE

8. What is the purpose of the "IN BOOLEAN MODE" modifier in a Full-Text Search query?

a. It specifies the language for the search query.

b. It forces an exact match search.
c. It performs a Boolean search with operators like +, -, and *.
d. It limits the search to a specific column.

9. In MySQL, which of the following data types can be used for Full-Text Search?
a. CHAR
b. VARCHAR
c. TEXT
d. INT

10. Which Boolean operator is used to require that a specific word appears in search results in MySQL Full-Text Search?
a. AND
b. OR
c. NOT
d. XOR

11. What does GIS stand for?
a. Global Information System
b. Geographical Information System
c. General Information System
d. Geographic Integrated System

12. In MySQL, which data type is commonly used to store spatial data, such as points, lines, and polygons?
a. INT
b. VARCHAR
c. BLOB
d. GEOMETRY

13. What is the purpose of the SRID (Spatial Reference ID) in spatial data?
a. It represents the shape of the Earth.
b. It defines the color of spatial data.
c. It specifies the coordinate system used to interpret the spatial data.
d. It denotes the data type of spatial objects.

14. Which MySQL function is used to check if a point is inside a polygon in a spatial query?
a. ST_CONTAINS
b. ST_INTERSECTS
c. ST_DISTANCE
d. ST_OVERLAPS

15. In MySQL, which data type is used to store JSON data?
a. JSON
b. TEXT
c. VARCHAR
d. BOOLEAN

16. Which JSON function is used to extract a specific value from a JSON object in MySQL?
a. JSON_SEARCH
b. JSON_EXTRACT
c. JSON_ARRAY
d. JSON_CONTAINS

17. What does the JSON_ARRAY function do in MySQL?
a. Returns a JSON object from a JSON array.
b. Returns a JSON array from a list of values.
c. Combines two JSON objects into a single object.
d. Checks if a value exists within a JSON array.

18. Which JSON function is used to determine if a JSON object contains a specific key in MySQL?
a. JSON_EXISTS
b. JSON_KEY
c. JSON_CONTAINS
d. JSON_SEARCH

19. In MySQL, which keyword is used to update a specific value in a JSON object?
a. UPDATE
b. MODIFY
c. SET
d. ALTER

20. What does the JSON_ARRAYAGG function do in MySQL?
a. Aggregates JSON arrays into a single JSON array.
b. Searches for a specific value within a JSON array.
c. Converts a JSON object into a JSON array.
d. Sorts a JSON array in ascending order.

21. What is a key-value store in the context of NoSQL features in MySQL?
a. A type of column in a relational table
b. A storage engine that stores data as key-value pairs
c. A type of NoSQL database in MySQL
d. A synonym for a primary key in MySQL
22. Which NoSQL storage engine is commonly used in MySQL for storing JSON documents?
a. InnoDB
b. MyISAM
c. NDB
d. JSON
23. What is the primary advantage of using the JSON data type in MySQL?
a. It enforces data consistency and integrity.
b. It allows for flexible and schema-less data storage.
c. It supports advanced querying and indexing.
d. It provides built-in support for ACID transactions.
24. How can you create a JSON document in MySQL?
a. Use the CREATE JSON statement.
b. Insert a JSON string using INSERT INTO.
c. Use the JSON_OBJECT function to create a JSON object.
d. Define a JSON data type column in a table.
25. Which SQL function is used to extract a specific attribute from a JSON document in MySQL?
a. JSON_PATH
b. JSON_EXTRACT
c. JSON_QUERY
d. JSON_MODIFY

Answer

1) c. 2) b. 3) a. 4) c. 5) c. 6) b. 7) b. 8) c. 9) c. 10) a. 11) b. 12) d. 13) c. 14) a. 15) a. 16) b. 17) b. 18) a. 19) c. 20) a. 21) b. 22) a. 23) b. 24) c. 25) b. 26) a. 27) b. 28) b. 29) b. 30) a.

ONLINE RESOURCES

Practice Paper
Link: https://forms.gle/DXLE6MaghS6b4R7A7
QR Code:

Video Content:
Link: https://www.youtube.com/playlist?list=PLzlh_31VWEFrNXWdsOnKsF5bIRE8CTJmA
QR Code:

12.1 Integrating MySQL with PHP

Integrating MySQL with PHP is a common task for web development, as it allows you to store and retrieve data from a MySQL database using PHP scripts. Here's an example of how to integrate MySQL with PHP:

Step 1: Setting Up Your Environment

Install MySQL: Make sure you have MySQL installed on your server or local development environment.

Install PHP: Ensure PHP is installed. You can use PHP along with a web server like Apache or Nginx.

Install MySQLi Extension: You'll need the MySQLi extension for PHP to interact with MySQL. You can enable it in your PHP configuration or install it as a separate package.

Step 2: Creating a MySQL Database

Let's create a simple MySQL database with a table to store user information. You can use the MySQL command-line client or a tool like phpMyAdmin to create the database and table.

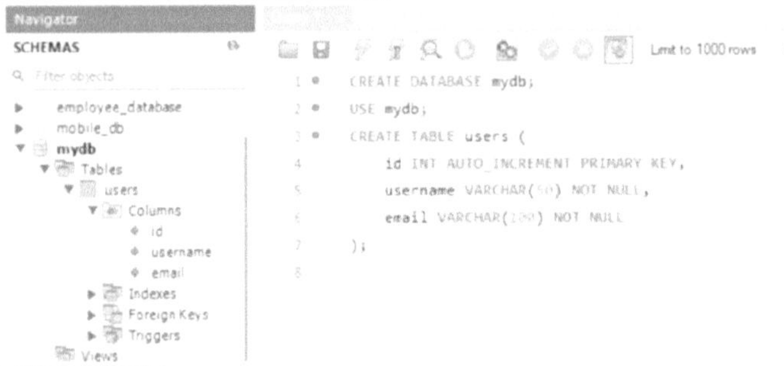

Step 3: Connecting to MySQL in PHP

In your PHP script, you'll need to establish a connection to the MySQL database. Here's an example of connecting to MySQL using the MySQLi extension:

```
<?php
$host = "localhost"; // MySQL host
$user = "username"; // MySQL username
$pass = "password"; // MySQL password
$db = "mydb"; // Database name

// Create a connection to MySQL
$mysqli = new mysqli($host, $user, $pass, $db);

// Check the connection
if ($mysqli->connect_error) {
    die("Connection failed: " . $mysqli->connect_error);
}
?>
```

Replace **"localhost"**, **"username"**, **"password"**, and **"mydb"** with your MySQL server details.

Step 4: Inserting Data into the Database

Let's insert some data into the **users** table:

```
<?php
// Sample data
$username = "john_doe";
$email = "john@example.com";

// SQL query to insert data
$sql = "INSERT INTO users (username, email) VALUES ('$username', '$email')";

// Execute the query
if ($mysqli->query($sql) === TRUE) {
    echo "Record inserted successfully.";
} else {
    echo "Error: " . $sql . "<br>" . $mysqli->error;
}
?>
```

Step 5: Retrieving Data from the Database

You can fetch data from the database using SQL queries. Here's an example of retrieving user data:

```
<?php
// SQL query to retrieve data
$sql = "SELECT id, username, email FROM users";
```

```
$result = $mysqli->query($sql);

if ($result->num_rows > 0) {
    while ($row = $result->fetch_assoc()) {
        echo "ID: " . $row["id"] . "<br>";
        echo "Username: " . $row["username"] . "<br>";
        echo "Email: " . $row["email"] . "<br><br>";
    }
} else {
    echo "No records found.";
}
?>
```

Closing the Connection

After you're done with database operations, close the MySQL connection to release resources:

```
<?php
$mysqli->close();
?>
```

That's a basic example of integrating MySQL with PHP. You can expand on this foundation to build more complex database-driven web applications. Make sure to use prepared statements and sanitize user inputs to prevent SQL injection and ensure security in your PHP and MySQL interactions.

12.2 MySQL and Python

Integrating MySQL with Python is a common task in web development, data analysis, and various applications. You can use the MySQL Connector/Python library (also known as MySQLdb) to interact with MySQL databases using Python. Here's how to get started with MySQL and Python:

Step 1: Install the MySQL Connector/Python Library

To use MySQL in Python, you need to install the MySQL Connector/Python library. You can install it using pip, the Python package manager:

pip install mysql-connector-python

Step 2: Connecting to a MySQL Database

Now that you have the library installed, you can establish a connection to your MySQL database. Make sure you have MySQL installed and a database set up.

```
import mysql.connector

# Define the database connection parameters
config = {
    "host": "localhost",
    "user": "your_username",
    "password": "your_password",
    "database": "your_database"
}

# Create a connection
conn = mysql.connector.connect(**config)

if conn.is_connected():
    print("Connected to MySQL")
else:
    print("Connection failed")
```

Replace **"localhost"**, **"your_username"**, **"your_password"**, and **"your_database"** with your MySQL server details.

Step 3: Executing SQL Queries

You can execute SQL queries using the MySQL Connector/Python library. Here's an example of inserting data into a MySQL table:

```
# Create a cursor to execute SQL queries
cursor = conn.cursor()

# SQL query to insert data
sql = "INSERT INTO your_table (column1, column2) VALUES (%s, %s)"

# Data to insert
data = ("value1", "value2")

# Execute the query
cursor.execute(sql, data)
```

```
# Commit the changes to the database
conn.commit()

# Close the cursor
cursor.close()
```

Step 4: Retrieving Data from the Database

You can retrieve data from the database using SQL queries and fetch methods. Here's an example of retrieving data from a MySQL table:

```
# Create a cursor
cursor = conn.cursor()

# SQL query to retrieve data
sql = "SELECT * FROM your_table"

# Execute the query
cursor.execute(sql)

# Fetch and print the results
results = cursor.fetchall()
for row in results:
    print(row)

# Close the cursor
cursor.close()
```

Step 5: Closing the Connection

After you finish working with the database, it's essential to close the connection to release resources:

```
# Close the database connection
conn.close()
```

Step 6: Error Handling

Make sure to add error handling to your code to deal with potential exceptions that might occur during database operations. Here's a basic example of integrating MySQL with Python. You can use this foundation to build more complex database-driven applications, perform data analysis, or create web services that interact with MySQL databases. Remember to handle exceptions, validate user inputs, and follow best practices for database security.

12.3 MySQL and JavaScript

MySQL and JavaScript are commonly used together in web development to create dynamic and interactive web applications. JavaScript, running on the client-side, can interact with MySQL, which typically runs on the server-side, to retrieve and manipulate data. This interaction is often facilitated through APIs and AJAX requests. Here's an overview of how MySQL and JavaScript can work together:

1. Server-Side Scripting:

MySQL is typically accessed and manipulated on the server-side of web applications. Server-side scripts (e.g., PHP, Python, Node.js) handle database operations and interact with MySQL.

2. APIs:

To enable communication between JavaScript (client-side) and MySQL (server-side), you can create APIs using server-side programming languages. These APIs receive requests from JavaScript and interact with the database accordingly.

3. AJAX (Asynchronous JavaScript and XML):

AJAX is a technology that allows JavaScript to make asynchronous requests to the server. With AJAX, you can fetch data from MySQL and update parts of a web page without needing to reload the entire page.

Here's a basic example of using JavaScript and AJAX to interact with MySQL through a server-side API:

Server-Side (e.g., Node.js):

```
const express = require('express');
const mysql = require('mysql');
const app = express();

// Create a MySQL connection
const connection = mysql.createConnection({
  host: 'localhost',
  user: 'your_username',
  password: 'your_password',
  database: 'your_database',
});

// Connect to MySQL
```

```
connection.connect((err) => {
  if (err) {
    console.error('MySQL connection failed: ' + err.stack);
    return;
  }
  console.log('Connected to MySQL as ID ' + connection.threadId);
});

// Define an API route to retrieve data from MySQL
app.get('/api/data', (req, res) => {
  const sql = 'SELECT * FROM your_table';
  connection.query(sql, (error, results, fields) => {
    if (error) {
      console.error('MySQL query error: ' + error.message);
      res.status(500).json({ error: 'Error retrieving data from MySQL' });
      return;
    }
    res.json(results);
  });
});

app.listen(3000, () => {
  console.log('Server is running on port 3000');
});
```

Client-Side (JavaScript):

```
<!DOCTYPE html>
<html>
<head>
  <title>MySQL and JavaScript</title>
</head>
<body>
  <button id="fetchData">Fetch Data from MySQL</button>
  <ul id="dataList"></ul>

  <script>
    const fetchDataButton = document.getElementById('fetchData');
    const dataList = document.getElementById('dataList');

    fetchDataButton.addEventListener('click', () => {
      // Make an AJAX request to the server-side API
      fetch('/api/data')
        .then(response => response.json())
        .then(data => {
          dataList.innerHTML = '';
          data.forEach(item => {
            const li = document.createElement('li');
            li.textContent = item.name; // Adjust this based on the structure of your MySQL data
            dataList.appendChild(li);
          });
        })
        .catch(error => console.error('AJAX error: ' + error));
    });
  </script>
</body>
</html>
```

In this example, a Node.js server serves as the server-side application, providing an API for retrieving data from MySQL. On the client-side, JavaScript is used to make an AJAX request to the API and update the web page dynamically. This demonstrates the basic flow of how JavaScript can interact with MySQL in a web application.

12.4 Building Web Applications with MySQL

Building web applications with MySQL is a common practice in web development. MySQL is used as the database management system to store, manage, and retrieve data for web applications. Here are the key steps and components involved in building web applications with MySQL:

Requirements Gathering and Planning:

Determine the goals and requirements of your web application, including the type of data it will manage, the user interactions, and the features to be implemented.

Database Design:

Design the database schema, including tables, columns, relationships, and data types. Use tools like MySQL Workbench to create and visualize your database schema.

MySQL Setup:

Install and configure MySQL on your server or local development environment. Create a MySQL user with appropriate privileges for your application.

Server-Side Programming:

Choose a server-side programming language such as PHP, Python, Node.js, Ruby, or Java to interact with the MySQL database. Create server-side scripts to handle HTTP requests, process data, and communicate with the database.

Establishing a Database Connection:

Use the MySQL Connector/Driver for your chosen programming language to establish a connection to the MySQL database. Provide the necessary credentials to connect securely.

Create APIs:

Develop APIs (Application Programming Interfaces) to expose database functionality to the front-end. These APIs handle CRUD (Create, Read, Update, Delete) operations and enable data retrieval and manipulation.

User Authentication and Authorization:

Implement user authentication and authorization to secure your web application. MySQL can store user credentials and roles, which can be used to control access to certain parts of the application.

Building the Front-End:

Develop the user interface (UI) of your web application using HTML, CSS, and JavaScript. Use frameworks like React, Angular, or Vue.js for dynamic and interactive front-ends.

AJAX and Data Exchange:

Use AJAX (Asynchronous JavaScript and XML) or modern fetch APIs in JavaScript to communicate with the server-side APIs. This allows for real-time data updates without reloading the entire page.

Form Handling:

Create forms for user input and data submission. Validate user input on both the client and server sides to prevent security vulnerabilities.

Data Validation and Sanitization:

Ensure that data sent to and received from the database is properly validated and sanitized to prevent SQL injection and other security risks.

Error Handling:

Implement robust error handling and reporting to gracefully handle unexpected issues or invalid user inputs.

Testing:

Conduct thorough testing of your web application, including unit testing, integration testing, and user acceptance testing.

Deployment:

Deploy your web application to a production server or a web hosting service. Configure the production database connection settings.

Performance Optimization:

Optimize database queries, use indexing, and implement caching to improve the application's performance.

Security Considerations:

Regularly update and patch your MySQL server to protect against security vulnerabilities. Implement SSL for secure data transmission. Encrypt sensitive data in the database.

Backups and Disaster Recovery:

Set up regular database backups and disaster recovery procedures to protect against data loss.

Scalability:

Plan for scalability by using appropriate MySQL storage engines, horizontal scaling techniques, and load balancing for high-traffic applications.

Monitoring and Logging:

Implement monitoring and logging to track application usage, database performance, and potential security breaches.

Documentation:

Document your web application, database schema, and API endpoints for future reference and collaboration with other developers.

Building web applications with MySQL involves a combination of database design, server-side programming, and front-end development. It's important to follow best practices for security, scalability, and performance to create robust and reliable applications. Additionally, staying up-to-date with MySQL updates and security patches is crucial for maintaining a secure database system.

12.5 Exercise

1. What does MySQL stand for in the context of PHP and databases?

a. My Structured Query Language

b. MySQL Query Language

c. My Structured Query Library
d. None of the above
2. Which PHP function is commonly used to establish a connection to a MySQL database?
a. connect()
b. mysql_connect()
c. mysqli_connect()
d. db_connect()
3. What is the purpose of the MySQLi extension in PHP?
a. It allows you to interact with MySQL databases using Object-Oriented programming.
b. It's used to create HTML forms for user input.
c. It manages PHP session variables.
d. It's used for sending email via PHP.
4. Which PHP function is used to execute a MySQL query and fetch the result?
a. execute()
b. query()
c. fetch()
d. mysql_query()
5. What is the primary advantage of using prepared statements in PHP when working with MySQL databases?
a. Improved database security by preventing SQL injection.
b. Faster execution of SQL queries.
c. Simpler and more concise code.
d. Enhanced compatibility with other database systems.
6. Which of the following is not a valid method for handling errors when connecting to a MySQL database in PHP?
a. die()
b. try...catch block
c. error_reporting()
d. or_die()
7. Which PHP function is used to retrieve a single row of data from a MySQL query result?
a. fetch_row()
b. fetch_assoc()
c. fetch_array()
d. fetch_object()
8. What is the purpose of the mysql_real_escape_string() function in PHP?
a. It encrypts data before storing it in a MySQL database.
b. It converts special characters to their HTML entities.
c. It escapes characters to make them safe for use in SQL queries to prevent SQL injection.
d. It retrieves data from a MySQL database.
9. In a MySQL database, what is the role of a primary key?
a. It ensures that the database is secure and encrypted.
b. It prevents unauthorized users from accessing the data.
c. It uniquely identifies each record in a table.
d. It helps in creating complex SQL queries.
10. Which of the following PHP functions is used to close a connection to a MySQL database?
a. disconnect()
b. close()
c. mysqli_close()
d. mysql_close()
11. What is MySQL?
a. A programming language
b. A relational database management system (RDBMS)
c. A web framework
d. A Python library
12. Which of the following is NOT a valid data type in MySQL?
a. INT
b. FLOAT
c. STRING
d. DATE
13. What Python library is commonly used to interact with MySQL databases?
a. PyMySQL

b. SQLAlchemy
c. Django
d. SQLite
14. In MySQL, which SQL statement is used to create a new database?
a. CREATE TABLE
b. CREATE DATABASE
c. CREATE SCHEMA
d. CREATE INDEX
15. What is the default port number for MySQL server?
a. 3306
b. 5432
c. 80
d. 8080
16. Which Python module is used to connect to a MySQL database and execute SQL queries?
a. mysql-connector
b. database-connector
c. sql-connect
d. mysql-python
17. What command is used in MySQL to retrieve all records from a table?
a. SELECT *
b. SELECT ALL
c. RETRIEVE *
d. FETCH ALL
18. Which statement is used to delete a record from a MySQL table?
a. DELETE
b. DROP
c. REMOVE
d. ERASE
19. In Python, how can you protect your MySQL database from SQL injection attacks when executing SQL queries?
a. Use prepared statements or parameterized queries
b. Increase the database password complexity
c. Use a firewall
d. Rename the database tables
20. Which Python library is commonly used for Object-Relational Mapping (ORM) when working with MySQL databases?
a. SQLAlchemy
b. PyMySQL
c. SQLite
d. Django
21. What is the role of MySQL in web applications?
a) Front-end scripting
b) Database management
c) User interface design
d) Server-side scripting
22. Which of the following is not a valid data type in MySQL?
a) INT
b) VARCHAR
c) BOOLEAN
d) DATETIME
23. In a web application, which component is responsible for executing server-side code and interacting with the database?
a) HTML
b) JavaScript
c) CSS
d) Server
24. Which JavaScript function is commonly used to make asynchronous requests to a MySQL database from a web page?
a) connect()
b) fetch()
c) query()
d) load()
25. What is the purpose of a SQL query in the context of a web application with MySQL?

a) Define the web page layout
b) Retrieve or manipulate data in the database
c) Style the web page elements
d) Handle user interactions

26. Which JavaScript framework is often used for building interactive web applications that communicate with MySQL databases?
a) React
b) Angular
c) Vue.js
d) jQuery

27. In MySQL, what does the SELECT statement do?
a) Insert data into a table
b) Delete data from a table
c) Retrieve data from a table
d) Update data in a table

28. Which of the following is a common method of securing a web application's interaction with a MySQL database?
a) Using plain text for database passwords
b) Implementing proper user authentication
c) Running the MySQL server without a password
d) Storing database credentials in JavaScript files

29. What is the purpose of using AJAX in web applications?
a) To create stylish user interfaces
b) To manage server-side logic
c) To make asynchronous requests to the server
d) To prevent SQL injection attacks

30. Which of the following is NOT a benefit of using JavaScript to interact with a MySQL database in a web application?
a) Improved user experience through real-time updates
b) Enhanced security by storing database credentials in JavaScript files
c) Faster loading times by loading data on-demand
d) Reduced server load through asynchronous communication

Answer

1) c. 2) c. 3) a. 4) b. 5) a. 6) d. 7) b. 8) c. 9) c. 10) c. 11) b. 12) c. 13) a. 14) b. 15) a. 16) a. 17) a. 18) a. 19) a. 20) a. 21) b. 22) c. 23) d. 24) b. 25) b. 26) a. 27) c. 28) b. 29) c. 30) b.

ONLINE RESOURCES

Practice Paper
Link: https://forms.gle/rbP6XoKETkscLiC7A
QR Code:

Video Content:
Link: https://www.youtube.com/playlist?list=PLzlh_31VWEFpXHvD6vus_FDFpsRLkzjxf
QR Code:

13.1 Deploying MySQL in the Cloud

Deploying MySQL in the cloud is a popular choice for many organizations as it offers scalability, flexibility, and cost-effectiveness. Cloud providers like Amazon Web Services (AWS), Microsoft Azure, and Google Cloud Platform (GCP) offer managed database services that make it easier to deploy and manage MySQL in the cloud. Here's a detailed overview of how to deploy MySQL in the cloud, specifically using AWS as an example:

Step 1: Sign Up for a Cloud Provider:

If you don't already have an account, sign up for a cloud provider like AWS. You'll need to provide payment information, create an account, and set up a billing method.

Step 2: Choose a Cloud Service:

Most cloud providers offer managed database services. In AWS, you can use Amazon RDS (Relational Database Service) to deploy MySQL. In GCP, you can use Cloud SQL, and in Azure, you can use Azure Database for MySQL.

Step 3: Create a MySQL Instance:

In AWS, navigate to the Amazon RDS console and click "Create database." Select MySQL as the database engine.

Step 4: Configure Database Settings:

Specify your database details, including the instance size, storage, database name, and master username and password. Configure your network settings, including VPC (Virtual Private Cloud), security groups, and subnets.

Step 5: Choose Advanced Settings:

Configure additional options, such as parameter groups, automatic backups, maintenance windows, and enhanced monitoring.

Step 6: Review and Launch:

Review your settings, make any necessary adjustments, and click "Create database." The cloud provider will set up your MySQL instance.

Step 7: Access Your MySQL Instance:

Once your MySQL instance is created, you can access it using the provided endpoint, username, and password. You can use tools like MySQL Workbench or the command line to connect to your database.

Step 8: Data Migration:

If you have an existing MySQL database, you'll need to migrate your data to the cloud. Most cloud providers offer tools and documentation to help you with data migration.

Step 9: Security and Access Control:

Set up security measures like SSL certificates and IAM (Identity and Access Management) policies to control access to your MySQL instance. Ensure your cloud environment follows security best practices.

Step 10: Monitor and Optimize:

Use the monitoring and logging tools provided by your cloud provider to keep an eye on database performance. Adjust instance sizes, storage, and configurations as needed to optimize performance and cost.

Example: Deploying MySQL on AWS (Amazon RDS):

Here's a more detailed example of deploying MySQL on AWS using Amazon RDS:

Sign in to AWS: Log in to your AWS account.

Navigate to RDS: In the AWS Management Console, go to the Amazon RDS dashboard.

Create Database: Click the "Create database" button.

Select Engine: Choose "MySQL" as the database engine.

Specify Details: Fill in database details, such as DB instance identifier, master username, and password. Configure instance class, storage, and network settings.

Additional Configuration: Configure advanced settings like parameter groups, backup and maintenance options, and database options.

Security: Set up security groups, VPC settings, and specify who can access the database.

Create Database: Review your settings, and click "Create database."

Access Your Database: Once the database is created, you can access it using the provided endpoint, username, and password.

Data Migration: Migrate your data from your local MySQL server to the Amazon RDS instance.

Security and Access Control: Configure SSL, IAM, and other security measures.

Monitoring and Optimization: Use AWS CloudWatch and database performance insights to monitor and optimize your MySQL instance.

Deploying MySQL in the cloud simplifies database management, provides scalability, and offers built-in backups and high availability features. However, it's essential to follow best practices, monitor your database's performance, and regularly update your cloud-based MySQL instance for security and efficiency.

13.2 Amazon RDS for MySQL

Amazon RDS (Relational Database Service) for MySQL is a managed database service provided by Amazon Web Services (AWS). It simplifies the process of setting up, operating, and scaling a MySQL relational database in the cloud. Here's an overview of Amazon RDS for MySQL:

Key Features and Benefits:

Managed Service: Amazon RDS automates database management tasks like patching, backups, and replication, allowing you to focus on your applications rather than database maintenance.
MySQL Compatibility: It fully supports MySQL, which means your existing MySQL applications can run on Amazon RDS without modification.
Scalability: You can easily scale your database up or down by changing the instance type to accommodate changes in traffic and storage requirements.
High Availability: Amazon RDS for MySQL offers Multi-AZ deployments with automatic failover to enhance availability and data durability. It also provides read replicas for improved read performance.
Automated Backups: Amazon RDS automatically takes daily backups of your database, which can be retained for a specified duration. You can also take manual snapshots for point-in-time recovery.
Security: It provides features like encryption at rest and in transit, IAM (Identity and Access Management) integration, and security groups to control network access to your RDS instances.
Monitoring and Logging: Amazon RDS offers CloudWatch integration for monitoring database performance, and you can set up alarms for automated responses to issues. It also supports database logs for troubleshooting.
Scalable Storage: You can easily increase your database storage capacity as needed, and it offers high-performance storage options.
Database Engine Upgrades: Amazon RDS allows for easy upgrades to new MySQL versions with minimal downtime.
Creating an Amazon RDS for MySQL Instance:
Here's a simplified overview of the process to create an Amazon RDS for MySQL instance:
Sign in to AWS: Log in to your AWS account.
Navigate to RDS: Access the Amazon RDS service in the AWS Management Console.
Create Database: Click the "Create database" button.
Select Engine: Choose "MySQL" as the database engine.
Specify Details: Fill in database details, such as DB instance identifier, master username, and password. Configure instance class, storage, and network settings.
Additional Configuration: Configure advanced settings like parameter groups, backup and maintenance options, and database options.
Security: Set up security groups, VPC settings, and specify who can access the database.
Create Database: Review your settings, and click "Create database."
Access Your Database: Once the database is created, you can access it using the provided endpoint, username, and password.
Use Cases:
Amazon RDS for MySQL is suitable for a wide range of use cases, including:
Web Applications: Hosting the backend database for websites and web applications.
E-commerce: Managing product catalogs, order processing, and user data.
Content Management Systems (CMS): Storing and managing content for CMS platforms like WordPress and Drupal.
Business Applications: Handling data for CRM systems, HR management, and inventory management.
Analytics and Reporting: Supporting business intelligence and reporting applications.
Log Management: Storing and analyzing log data for monitoring and troubleshooting.
Best Practices:
To make the most of Amazon RDS for MySQL, consider following these best practices:
Regularly update your database to the latest MySQL version.
Set up automated backups and test your ability to restore data from backups.
Implement monitoring and alerting to track performance and address issues proactively.
Use Multi-AZ deployments for high availability.
Encrypt your data both at rest and in transit.
Optimize your database by adjusting parameter groups and index design for performance.
Amazon RDS for MySQL simplifies database management in the AWS cloud environment, making it a popular choice for organizations looking to leverage the benefits of a managed MySQL database service.

13.3 Google Cloud SQL

Google Cloud SQL is a fully managed relational database service provided by Google Cloud Platform (GCP). It offers a convenient and scalable way to run and manage relational databases in the cloud. Google Cloud SQL supports various database engines, including MySQL, PostgreSQL, and SQL Server. In this overview, we'll focus on Google Cloud SQL for MySQL.
Key Features and Benefits:
Managed Service: Google Cloud SQL automates database management tasks such as backups, patch management, and replication, reducing the operational overhead.
High Availability: It offers built-in high availability with automatic failover, reducing downtime and ensuring data reliability.
Scalability: You can easily scale your database vertically by changing the instance size or horizontally by adding read replicas to handle increased traffic.
Security: Google Cloud SQL provides multiple layers of security, including encryption at rest and in transit, identity and access management (IAM) integration, and network security through VPC (Virtual Private Cloud) peering.

Automated Backups: Regular automated backups are performed, and you can restore your database to any point within the backup retention period.
Performance Monitoring: Google Cloud SQL integrates with Google Cloud Monitoring and Logging, allowing you to monitor and analyze database performance, set up alerts, and review logs.
Geo-replication: It supports cross-region read replicas for improved read performance and disaster recovery.
Database Migration: Google Cloud SQL offers tools and services to simplify database migration from on-premises or other cloud providers.
Creating a Google Cloud SQL for MySQL Instance:
Here's a simplified overview of the process to create a Google Cloud SQL for MySQL instance:
Sign in to GCP: Log in to your Google Cloud Platform account.
Navigate to SQL: Access the Google Cloud SQL service in the GCP Console.
Create Instance: Click the "Create Instance" button.
Select Database Engine: Choose "MySQL" as the database engine.
Specify Details: Fill in instance details, such as instance ID, root password, and location. Configure machine type, storage, and networking options.
Additional Configuration: Set up advanced settings, including database flags, automatic backups, and maintenance preferences.
Connectivity: Configure security settings, including authorized networks and SSL certificates.
Create Instance: Review your settings and click "Create" to provision your Google Cloud SQL instance.
Use Cases:
Google Cloud SQL is suitable for various use cases, including:
Web Applications: Hosting the database backend for web applications and websites.
E-commerce: Managing product catalogs, order processing, and customer data.
Content Management Systems (CMS): Storing and managing content for platforms like WordPress and Joomla.
Business Applications: Handling data for CRM systems, ERP, and financial applications.
Development and Testing: Creating and managing development and testing databases.
Analytics: Supporting analytics and reporting applications.
Best Practices:
To make the most of Google Cloud SQL for MySQL, consider following these best practices:
Regularly update your database to the latest MySQL version.
Set up automated backups and test your ability to restore data from backups.
Implement monitoring and alerting to track performance and address issues proactively.
Use read replicas to offload read traffic and improve query performance.
Encrypt your data both at rest and in transit.
Optimize your database by adjusting database flags and index design for performance.
Google Cloud SQL for MySQL offers a managed, highly available, and scalable database solution that's well-suited for a wide range of applications and workloads in the Google Cloud environment.

13.4 Microsoft Azure Database for MySQL

Microsoft Azure Database for MySQL is a managed database service provided by Microsoft Azure for running MySQL databases in the cloud. It offers a platform-as-a-service (PaaS) approach to database management, which simplifies database deployment, maintenance, and scalability. Here's an overview of Azure Database for MySQL:
Key Features and Benefits:
Managed Service: Azure Database for MySQL automates database management tasks, including updates, patching, backups, and monitoring, allowing you to focus on your applications.
MySQL Compatibility: It fully supports the MySQL database engine, which means your existing MySQL applications can run on Azure without modification.
High Availability: Azure Database for MySQL offers high availability options with automatic failover, ensuring that your applications experience minimal downtime.
Scalability: You can easily scale your database vertically by changing the compute and storage capacity, and you can also horizontally scale by adding read replicas to handle increased workloads.
Security: It provides robust security features, including encryption at rest and in transit, firewall rules, and Azure Active Directory integration for authentication.
Automated Backups: Azure Database for MySQL performs automated backups and allows you to restore your database to any point within the backup retention period.
Monitoring and Alerts: It integrates with Azure Monitor and Azure Security Center for performance monitoring, logging, and security analysis. You can set up alerts to receive notifications about database performance issues.
Geo-replication: You can configure geo-replication to create read replicas in different regions for improved read performance and disaster recovery.
Database Migration: Azure offers tools and services to simplify database migration, whether you are migrating from on-premises databases or other cloud providers.
Creating an Azure Database for MySQL Instance:
Here's a simplified overview of the process to create an Azure Database for MySQL instance:
Sign in to Azure: Log in to your Microsoft Azure account.

Create a New Database: Access the Azure portal and click "Create a resource." Search for "Azure Database for MySQL" and click "Create."
Basic Configuration: Specify basic settings, such as server name, authentication credentials, and subscription details.
Server Configuration: Configure server settings, such as resource group, location, compute and storage options.
Advanced Configuration: Set advanced settings, including backup retention, point-in-time restore, and security options.
Networking: Configure networking settings, such as firewall rules, virtual network integration, and public access.
Tags and Review: Optionally add tags for organization and review your settings.
Create: Click "Create" to provision your Azure Database for MySQL instance.
Use Cases:
Azure Database for MySQL is suitable for a variety of use cases, including:
Web Applications: It can serve as the database backend for web applications and websites.
Content Management Systems (CMS): Storing and managing content for platforms like WordPress and Joomla.
E-commerce: Managing product catalogs, order processing, and customer data for online stores.
Business Applications: Supporting CRM systems, ERP, and other business applications.
Development and Testing: Creating and managing databases for development and testing purposes.
Analytics and Reporting: Backing analytics and reporting applications with data storage.
Best Practices:
To make the most of Azure Database for MySQL, consider following these best practices:
Regularly update your database to the latest MySQL version.
Set up automated backups and test your ability to restore data from backups.
Implement monitoring and alerting to track performance and address issues proactively.
Use read replicas to offload read traffic and improve query performance.
Encrypt your data both at rest and in transit.
Optimize your database by fine-tuning query performance and indexing.
Azure Database for MySQL simplifies database management in the Azure cloud environment, offering a managed, highly available, and scalable database solution that's well-suited for various applications and workloads.

13.5 Exercise

1. What is Amazon RDS?
a. A relational database management system
b. A cloud-based data warehousing service
c. A content delivery network (CDN)
d. An open-source database system
2. Which cloud service provider offers Amazon RDS for MySQL?
a. Microsoft Azure
b. Google Cloud Platform
c. Amazon Web Services (AWS)
d. IBM Cloud
3. What is the primary benefit of using Amazon RDS for MySQL over managing your own MySQL database on EC2 instances?
a. Lower cost
b. Greater control and customization
c. Improved scalability and high availability
d. Faster data retrieval
4. In Amazon RDS for MySQL, what is the purpose of a Read Replica?
a. It's a backup of the database for disaster recovery.
b. It's used to manage database security.
c. It's used for read scaling and offloading read traffic.
d. It's a copy of the database schema for development purposes.
5. What is the maximum storage capacity for an Amazon RDS for MySQL instance?
a. 100 GB
b. 1 TB
c. 5 TB
d. 10 TB
6. Which Amazon RDS for MySQL feature allows you to automatically capture and store database backups for a specified retention period?
a. Data snapshots
b. Data warehousing
c. multi-AZ deployments
d. Automated backups
7. When you deploy Amazon RDS for MySQL, which authentication method is recommended for enhanced security?
a. Using a single, shared username and password for all users
b. Using IAM (Identity and Access Management) authentication
c. Allowing anonymous access to the database

d. Disabling authentication for improved performance
8. In Amazon RDS for MySQL, what does Multi-AZ (Availability Zone) deployment provide?
a. Improved write performance
b. Data partitioning for horizontal scalability
c. High availability and automatic failover to a standby instance in a different Availability Zone
d. Advanced reporting and analytics tools
9. What is the purpose of Parameter Groups in Amazon RDS for MySQL?
a. They are used to group database instances for load balancing.
b. They control the configuration settings for your database instance.
c. They are used for creating read replicas.
d. They are used to manage user access and permissions.
10. Which AWS service can be used for monitoring and managing the performance of your Amazon RDS for MySQL instances?
a. Amazon CloudFront
b. Amazon RDS Performance Insights
c. Amazon Redshift
d. Amazon S3
11. What are Google Cloud SQL and Microsoft Azure Database for MySQL?
a. Operating systems
b. Database management systems
c. Cloud storage services
d. Virtualization platforms
12. Which cloud provider offers Google Cloud SQL?
a. Amazon Web Services (AWS)
b. Google Cloud Platform (GCP)
c. Microsoft Azure
d. IBM Cloud
13. Which cloud provider offers Microsoft Azure Database for MySQL?
a. Amazon Web Services (AWS)
b. Google Cloud Platform (GCP)
c. Microsoft Azure
d. IBM Cloud
14. Google Cloud SQL and Microsoft Azure Database for MySQL both offer managed database services. What does "managed" mean in this context?
a. Users have full control over the database infrastructure.
b. The database service is maintained and operated by the cloud provider.
c. It's an open-source database system.
d. The database is hosted on-premises.
15. Which programming languages and frameworks are supported by Google Cloud SQL and Microsoft Azure Database for MySQL?
a. Only Python
b. Only JavaScript
c. Multiple languages and frameworks
d. No support for programming languages
16. Which of the following is not a key feature of Google Cloud SQL or Microsoft Azure Database for MySQL?
a. Automatic backups
b. High availability with automatic failover
c. Real-time data analytics
d. Scalability
17. Google Cloud SQL and Microsoft Azure Database for MySQL both support which query language?
a. SQL (Structured Query Language)
b. NoSQL
c. Python
d. Ruby
18. What is the primary purpose of using Google Cloud SQL or Microsoft Azure Database for MySQL?
a. Data storage
b. Virtual machine hosting
c. Container orchestration
d. Running machine learning models
19. Which of the following is true about data security in Google Cloud SQL and Microsoft Azure Database for MySQL?
a. Data security is not a concern in these services.
b. Both services provide built-in security features and encryption options.
c. Users are responsible for securing their own data.
d. These services are not suitable for storing sensitive data.

20. How can you scale your database in Google Cloud SQL and Microsoft Azure Database for MySQL to handle increased workloads?
a. Manually adjust the hardware of the underlying servers.
b. It's not possible to scale these databases.
c. Automatically add more resources as needed.
d. Delete data to reduce the workload.

Answer

1) a. 2) c. 3) c. 4) c. 5) c. 6) d. 7) b. 8) c. 9) b. 10) b. 11) b. 12) b. 13) c. 14) b. 15) c. 16) c. 17) a. 18) a. 19) b. 20) c.

ONLINE RESOURCES

Practice Paper
Link: https://forms.gle/5XJikzGpGih1wm2J7
QR Code:

Video Content:
Link: https://www.youtube.com/playlist?list=PLzlh_31VWEFrxU0fHSnKF1abVw4I0PLRQ
QR Code:

MySQL 8.0 Database Administration 1Z0-908

14.1 Introduction

Oracle Certifications are one of the most sought-after badges of proficiency in the Information Technology industry. An Oracle Certification shows that you have a thorough understanding of your professional responsibilities as well as MySQL products.

Oracle certifications on MySQL are used by consultants, developers, and DBAs to demonstrate to prospective employers and customers that they are up to date on the latest features, tools, and tricks.

MySQL 8.0 Database Developer Oracle Certified Professional

MySQL 8.0 Database Developer is a professional level certification that developers can earn through taking Oracle University's examination. This examination is designated to be "1Z0-909". Database developers requires such exams to evaluate upon the knowledge set and analyze the full set of requirements for being a skilled MySQL database developer.
An Oracle Certified Professional in MySQL 8.0 Database Developer certifies that the applicant has the necessary knowledge and abilities to use connectors and APIs, as well as how to support data-driven applications using the MySQL database. This certification verifies that the individual can design, create, and maintain MySQL schema objects, as well as manage transactions in SLQ and applications.

Exam Details

Certification Name	MySQL 8.0 Database Developer Oracle Certified Professional
Exam Name	1Z0-909
Format	Objective
Number of Questions	65
Duration	90 minutes
Passing Score	62%
Validation	Against the MySQL version 8.0

14.2 Exam Topics

Connectors and APIs

- Choosing between connectors for a given application
- Demonstrate the connector's use, management, and configuration
- Retrieving data from the given database by using a connector
- Handling special values
- Securing credentials and connections

Data-driven Applications

- Using prepared statements
- Setting SQL Modes for changing MySQL behaviour
- Handling and interpreting errors and warnings
- Displaying query results
- Aggregating and summarizing data
- Advanced Report Generation

MySQL Schema Objects and Data

- Designing, creating, and altering views
- Storing and processing string data
- Storing and processing numeric data
- Storing and processing temporal data
- Storing and processing spatial data

Transactions

- Controlling transactions in SQL
- Controlling transactions in applications
- Resolving consistency problems with isolation levels
- Understanding locking mechanisms within MySQL

Query Optimization

- Using indexes for optimization
- Analyzing queries for optimization
- Rewriting queries for optimization

MySQL Stored Programs

- Creating and executing stored routines
- Explaining the programming constructs used in stored routines
- Creating and executing triggers
- Scheduling database operations

JSON and Document Store

Creating and storing JSON documents
Processing data in JSON documents
Explaining application development with NoSQL and XDevAPI
Creating and accessing a document store
Using MySQL Shell for accessing document stores

14.3 Practice Questions and Answers

1. Examine this statement, which executes successfully:

You want to improve the performance of this query:

Which change enables the query to succeed while accessing fewer rows?
A. ALTER TABLE world.city ADD SPATIAL INDEX (Name);
B. ALTER TABLE world.city ADD SPATIAL INDEX (Population);
C. ALTER TABLE world.city ADD INDEX (Population);
D. ALTER TABLE world.city ADD INDEX (Name);
E. ALTER TABLE world.city ADD FULLTEXT INDEX (Name);
F. ALTER TABLE world.city ADD FULLTEXT INDEX (Population);

Correct Answer: B

2. A clean shutdown was performed with innodb_fast_shutdown=0.
While you were manipulating files, all files were accidentally deleted from the top-level data directory.
Which two files must be restored from backup to allow the DB to restart cleanly? (Choose two.)
A. ibtmp1
B. undo_001
C. ib_buffer_pool
D. ibdata1
E. mysql.ibd
F. ib_logfile0

Correct Answer: C, E

3. Which three are characteristics of a newly created role? (Choose three.)
A. It can be dropped using the DROP ROLE statement.
B. It is stored in the mysql.role table.
C. It is created as a locked account.
D. It can be renamed using the RENAME ROLE statement.
E. It can be granted to user accounts.
F. It can be protected with a password.

Correct Answer: A, E, F

4. You have configured GTID-based asynchronous replication with one master and one slave.
A user accidentally updated some data on the slave.
To fix this, you stopped replication and successfully reverted the accidental changes.
Examine the current GTID information:

You must fix GTID sets on the slave to avoid replicating unwanted transactions in case of failover.
Which set of actions would allow the slave to continue replicating without erroneous transactions?
A. RESET MASTER;
SET GLOBAL gtid_purged=aaaaaaaa-aaaa-aaaa-aaaa-aaaaaaaaaaaa:1-10167;
B.SET GLOBAL gtid_purged=aaaaaaaa-aaaa-aaaa-aaaa-aaaaaaaaaaaa:1-2312,bbbbbbbb-bbbb-bbbb-bbbb-bbbbbbbbbbbb:1-9;
SET GLOBAL gtid_executed=aaaaaaaa-aaaa-aaaa-aaaa-aaaaaaaaaaaa:1-10167;
C. RESET SLAVE;
SET GLOBAL gtid_purged=aaaaaaaa-aaaa-aaaa-aaaa-aaaaaaaaaaaa:1-3820;
SET GLOBAL gtid_executed=aaaaaaaa-aaaa-aaaa-aaaa—aaaaaaaaaaaa:1-10300;
D. RESET MASTER;
SET GLOBAL gtid_purged-aaaaaaaa-aaaa-aaaa-aaaa-aaaaaaaaaaaa:1-2312;
SET GLOBAL gtid_executed=aaaaaaaa-aaaa-aaaa-aaaa-aaaaaaaaaaaa:1-10167;
E. RESET SLAVE;
SET GLOBAL gtid_purged=aaaaaaaa-aaaa-aaaa-aaaa-aaaaaaaaaaaa:1-10167;

Correct Answer: D

5. Which two statements are true about the mysqld-auto.cnf file? (Choose two.)
A. This file is for storing MySQL Server configuration options in JSON format.
B. This file is for logging purposes only and is never processed.
C. It is read and processed at the beginning of startup configuration.
D. It is read and processed at the end of startup configuration.
E. It is always updated with changes to system variables.
F. This file is for storing MySQL server_uuid values only.
Correct Answer: D, E

6. The data in this instance is transient; no backup or replication will be required. It is currently under performing.
The database size is static and including indexes is 19G.
Total system memory is 32G.
After profiling the system, you highlight these MySQL status and global variables:

The OS metrics indicate that disk is a bottleneck.
Other variables retain their default values.
Which three changes will provide the most benefit to the instance? (Choose three.)
A. innodb_flush_log_at_trx_commit=1
B. buffer_pool_size=24G
C. innodb_log_file_size=1G
D. sync_binlog=0
E. innodb_doublewrite=0
F. max_connections=10000
G. innodb_undo_directory=/dev/shm
Correct Answer: A, C, F

7. You are considering using file-system snapshots to back up MySQL.
Which three statements are true? (Choose three.)
A. They take roughly twice as long as logical backups.
B. They allow direct copying of table rows with operating system copy commands.
C. They work best for transaction storage engines that can perform their own recovery when restored.
D. The backup window is almost zero from the perspective of the application.
E. They do not back up views, stored procedures, or configuration files.
F. There is a slight performance cost while the snapshot is active.
G. They do not use additional disk space.

8. What are three typical causes of MySQL becoming suddenly slow and unavailable?
(Choose three.)
A. A configuration change was made.
B. The hardware includes a single point of failure.
C. Monitoring has not enabled all Performance Schema instruments.
D. The MySQL Query Cache is disabled.
E. OPTIMIZE TABLE is not executes for the InnoDB tables.
F. The application executes a new untested query
Correct Answer: A, B, F

9. Which statement is true about InnoDB persistent index statistics?
A. Updating index statistics is an I/O expensive operation.
B. Index statistics are calculated from pages buffered in the buffer pool for tables with InnoDB storage engine.
C. Setting innodb_stats_auto_recalc=ON causes statistics to be updated automatically when a new index is created.
D. Execution plans based on transient index statistics improve precision when innodb_stats_persistent_sample_pages is increased.
E. Increasing innodb_stats_persistent_sample_pages determines higher pages scanning speed, at the cost of increased memory usage.
F. Tables are scanned and index statistics recalculated when an instance is restarted.
Correct Answer: D

10. Which two are features of MySQL Enterprise Firewall? (Choose two.)
A. recording incoming SQL statement to facilitate the creation of a whitelist of permitted commands
B. blocking of potential threats by configuring pre-approved whitelists
C. modifying SQL statement dynamically with substitutions
D. automatic locking of user accounts who break your firewall
E. provides stateless firewall access to TCP/3306

Correct Answer: B, C

11. Examine the modified output:
Seconds_Behind_ Master value is steadily growing.
What are two possible causes? (Choose two.)
A. The master is most probably too busy to transmit data and the slave needs to wait for more data.
B. One or more large tables do not have primary keys.
C. This value shows only I/O latency and is not indicative of the size of the transaction queue.
D. The master is producing a large volume of events in parallel but the slave is processing them serially.
E. The parallel slave threads are experiencing lock contention.

Correct Answer: C, D

12. You must configure the MySQL command-line client to provide the highest level of trust and security when connecting to a remote MySQL Server.
Which value of --ssl-mode will do this?
A. PREFERRED
B. VERIFY_CA
C. REQUIRED
D. VERIFY_IDENTITY
Correct Answer: C

13. Which three sets of item information are visible in the mysql system database? (Choose three.)
A. help topics
B. performance monitoring information
C. plugins
D. information about table structures
E. audit log events
F. rollback segments
G. time zone information and definitions

Correct Answer: A, C, F

14. You have a MySQL client installed on your Linux workstation with a default installation. You have your admin login credentials to connect to a MySQL server running Microsoft Windows on remote host 192.0.2.1:3306.
You wish to connect directly to the world database.
Which four options need to be specified to complete this task with a single command? (Choose four.)
A. -shared-memory-base-name-world
B. -protocol-UDP
C. -protocol-pipe
D. -password
E. -user-admin
F. -host-192.0.2.1
G. —socket=/tmp/mysql.sock
H. —database-world

Correct Answer: A, C, D, F

15. Consider this shell output and executed commands:
[root@oel7 ~]# ps aux | grep mysqld
mysql 2076 3.5 24.6 1386852 372572 ? Ssl 12:01 0:01 /usr/sbin/mysqid
[root@oel7 ~]# kill -15 2076
Which statement is true about MySQL server shutdown?
A. kill -15 should be avoided. Use other methods such as mysqladmin shutdown or systemctl stop mysqld.
B. kill -15 and kill -9 are effectively the same forced shutdown that risk committed transactions not written to disk.
C. kill -15 carries out a normal shutdown process, such as mysqladmin shutdown.
D. mysqld_safe prohibits commands that would harm the operation of the server. An error would be returned by the kill command.

Correct Answer: C

16. You wish to protect your MySQL database against SQL injection attacks.

Which method would fail to do this?
A. installing and configuring the Connection Control plugin
B. avoiding concatenation of SQL statements and user-supplied values in an application
C. using stored procedures for any database access
D. using PREPARED STATEMENTS
Correct Answer: C

17. You have just installed MySQL on Oracle Linux and adjusted your /etc/my.cnf parameters to suit your installation. Examine the output:

What statement is true about the start attempt?
A. MySQL server was not started due to a problem while executing process 2732.
B. MySQL server continued to start up even though another process existed.
C. systemd found the mysqld service disabled and failed to start it.
D. systemd waited for 30 seconds before timing out and start up failed.
E. systemd attempted to start mysqld, found another systemd mysqld process running, and shut it down.

Correct Answer: E

18. Examine these entries from the general query log:

All UPDATE statements reference existing rows.
Which describes the outcome of the sequence of statements?
A. Connection 24 experiences a lock wait timeout.
B. Connection 25 experiences a lock wait timeout.
C. A deadlock occurs immediately.
D. All statements execute without error.
E. A deadlock occurs after innodb_lock_wait_timeout seconds.

Correct Answer: E

19. Examine this command, which executes successfully:
$ mysqlrouter --bootstrap user@hostname:port --directory=directory_path
Which activity is performed?
A. MySQL Router is configured based on the information in files in directory_path.
B. MySQL Router configures itself based on the information retrieved from the InnoDB cluster metadata server.
C. MySQL Router is restarted.
D. MySQL Router configures all the cluster nodes based on the information retrieved from the InnoDB cluster metadata server.

Correct Answer: B

20. You encountered an insufficient privilege error in the middle of a long transaction.
The database administrator is informed and immediately grants the required privilege:
GRANT UPDATE ON world.city TO 'user1';
How can you proceed with your transaction with the least interruption?
A. Roll back the transaction and start the transaction again in the same session.
B. Re-execute the failed statement in your transaction.
C. Change the default database and re-execute the failed statement in your transaction.
D. Close the connection, reconnect, and start the transaction again.

Correct Answer: B

21. Examine these statements, which execute successfully:
CREATE ROLE r_world_rd;
GRANT SELECT ON world.* TO r_world_rd;
CREATE USER john IDENTIFIED BY 'P@ssw0rd';
GRANT r_world_rd TO john;
Examine these statements issued by user John:

What is the reason for the error?
A. The statement was blocked by MySQL Firewall.
B. John has not activated the role.
C. John needs to reconnect to the database.

D. The DBA needs to execute FLUSH PRIVILEGES.
Correct Answer: B

22. Binary log events for the 'mydb1' schema must be copied to a different schema name 'mydb2'. Which command will do this?
A. mysqlbinlog --rewrite-db='mydb1->mydb2' | mysql
B. mysqlbinlog --datebase=mydb1 --database=mydb2 | mysql
C. mysqlbinlog --rewrite-db='mydb1' --rewrite-db='mydb2' | mysql
D. mysqlbinlog --read-from-remote-server --raw | sed 's/mydb1/mydb2/g' | mysql

Correct Answer: D

23. Examine this MySQL Shell command:
dba.rebootClusterFromCompleteOutage()
Which two statements are true? (Choose two.)
A. It reconfigures InnoDB Cluster if the cluster was stopped.
B. It performs InnoDB Cluster instances rolling restart.
C. It only starts all InnoDB Cluster instances.
D. It is not mandatory that all instances are running and reachable before running the command.
E. It stops and restarts all InnoDB Cluster instances and initializes the metadata.
F. It only stops and restarts all InnoDB Cluster instances.
G. It picks the minimum number of instances necessary to rebuild the quorum and reconfigures InnoDB Cluster.

Correct Answer: B, D

24. Which two statements are true about MySQL server multi-source replication? (Choose two.)
A. It is not compatible with auto-positioning.
B. It needs to be re-instanced after a crash to maintain consistency.
C. It uses only time-based replication conflict resolution.
D. It relies on relay_log_recovery for resilient operations.
E. It does not attempt to detect or resolve replication conflicts.
F. It must use GTID replication.

Correct Answer: C, F

25. Which command enables rule-based MySQL Auditing capabilities?
A. shell> mysql < audit_log_filter_linux_install.sql
B. shell> mysqld --initialize --log-raw=audit.log
C. mysql> INSTALL PLUGIN audit_log;
D. mysql> INSTALL COMPONENT audit_log;

Correct Answer: A

26. Examine this SQL statement:
mysql> GRANT r_read@localhost TO mark WITH ADMIN OPTION;
Which two are true? (Choose two.)
A. Mark can grant the privileges assigned to the r_read@localhost role to another user.
B. ADMIN OPTION causes the role to be activated by default.
C. Mark can grant the r_read@localhost role to another user.
D. Mark can revoke the r_read@localhost role from another role.
E. ADMIN OPTION allows Mark to drop the role.
F. Mark must connect from localhost to activate the r_read@localhost role.

Correct Answer: AE

27. Which four are types of information stored in the MySQL data dictionary? (Choose four.)
A. performance metrics
B. table definitions
C. access control lists
D. view definitions
E. server runtime configuration
F. server configuration rollback
G. stored procedure definitions

H. InnoDB buffer pool LRU management data

Correct Answer: B, D, F, G

28. You have an InnoDB Cluster configured with three servers.
Examine this command, which executes successfully:
mysqldump -uroot -p -d mydatabase > mydatabase_backup.sql
Due to data loss, the cluster is initialized and a restore is attempted resulting in this error:
ERROR 13176 (HY000) at line 23: Cannot update GTID_PURGED with the Group Replication plugin running
Which two actions, either one of which, can fix this error and allow a successful restore of the cluster? (Choose two.)
A. Stop all instances except the primary read/write master instance and run the restore.
B. Remove the @@GLOBAL.gtid_purged statement from the dump file.
C. Create the backup by using the --set-gtid-purged=OFF option.
D. Remove the group replication plugin from each instance before restoring.
E. Remove the @@GLOBAL.gtid_executed statement from the dump file.
F. Restore using the --set-gtid-purged=OFF option.

Correct Answer: BC

29. Which statement is true about MySQL Enterprise Transparent Data Encryption (TDE)?
A. MySQL TDE uses an appropriate keyring plugin to store the keys in a centralized location.
B. Both MyISAM and InnoDB tables can be encrypted by setting the keyring_engine = ALL variable in the MySQL configuration file.
C. Lost tablespace encryption keys can be regenerated only if the master database key is known or present in the Key Vault specification.
D. TDE can encrypt InnoDB and MyISAM tables only when the tables are stored in the SYSTEM tablespace.

Correct Answer: C

30. You are upgrading a MySQL instance to the latest 8.0 version.
Examine this output:

You plan to add this parameter to the configuration:
innodb_directories='/innodb_extras'
Which statement is true?
A. It defines all innodb tablespace options relative to a starting parent directory.
B. It is not necessary because innodb_data_home_dir is already defined.
C. It allows scanning of other locations to discover more innodb tablespaces.
D. It moves all innodb tablespaces to the /innodb_extras directory to enable a new innodb_data_home_dir to be defined.
E. It adds more temporary workspace in addition to the innodb_tmpdir location.

Correct Answer: B

31. You wish to store the username and password for a client connection to MySQL server in a file on a local file system.
Which is the best way to encrypt the file?
A. Use the AES_ENCRYPT() MySQL function on the option file.
B. Use mysql_secure_installation to encrypt stored login credentials.
C. Use a text editor to create a new defaults file and encrypt it from Linux prompt.
D. Use mysql_config_editor to create an encrypted file.

Correct Answer: D
32. You are backing up raw InnoDB files by using mysqlbackup.
Which two groups of files will be backed up during a full backup? (Choose two.)
A. ibbackup files
B. *.CSM files
C. *.sdi files
D. *.ibd files
E. ib_logfile* files

Correct Answer: D, E

33. You made some table definition changes to a schema in your MySQL Server.
Which two statements reflect how MySQL Server handles the table definition changes? (Choose two.)
A. MySQL writes SDI to the binary log for distributed backups.

B. MySQL keeps InnoDB metadata changes in .sdi files in datadir.
C. The metadata is serialized in JSON format in Serialized Dictionary Information (SDI).
D. MySQL Server stores a copy of the serialized data in the InnoDB user tablespace.
E. MySQL implicitly executes FLUSH TABLES and stores a snapshot backup of the metadata.

Correct Answer: C, D

34. Which two are characteristics of snapshot-based backups? (Choose two.)
A. Snapshot-based backups greatly reduce time during which the database and applications are unavailable.
B. There is no need for InnoDB tables to perform its own recovery when restoring from the snapshot backup.
C. The frozen file system can be cloned to another virtual machine immediately into active service.
D. A separate physical copy must be made before releasing the snapshot backup.
E. Snapshot backups can be used only in virtual machines.

Correct Answer: D, E

35. You must run multiple instances of MySQL Server on a single host.
Which three methods are supported? (Choose three.)
A. Run MySQL Server docker containers.
B. Use systemd with different settings for each instance.
C. Use system tools to lock each instance to its own CPU.
D. Start mysqld or mysqld_safe using different option files for each instance.
E. Run mysqld with --datadir defined for each instance.
F. Use resource groups to lock different instances on separate CPUs.

Correct Answer: B, D, E

36. There are five MySQL instances configured with a working group replication.
Examine the output of the group members:

Which two statements are true about network partitioning in the cluster? (Choose two.)
A. The cluster will shut down to preserve data consistency.
B. The cluster has built-in high availability and updates group_replication_ip_whitelist to remove the unreachable nodes.
C. The group replication will buffer the transactions on the online nodes until the unreachable nodes return online.
D. There could be both a 2 node and 3 node group replication still running, so shutting down group replication and diagnosing the issue is recommended.
E. A manual intervention to force group members to be only the working two instances is required.

Correct Answer: A, B

37. Examine this statement and output:

You must try to reduce query execution time.
Which two queries should you focus on? (Choose two.)
A. QN = 3
B. QN = 5
C. QN = 1
D. QN = 4
E. QN = 2

Correct Answer: C, E

38. Examine this query:

What information does this query provide?
A. total memory used across all connections associated with the user on connection number 10
B. total memory used by the first 10 connections
C. total memory used by thread number 10
D. total memory used across all connections associated with the user on thread number 10
E. total memory used by connection number 10
F. total memory used by the first 10 threads

Correct Answer: E

39. On examination, your MySQL installation datadir has become recursively world read/write/executable.
What are two major concerns of running an installation with incorrect file privileges? (Choose two.)
A. Users could overwrite configuration files.
B. Data files could be deleted.
C. SQL injections could be used to insert bad data into the database.
D. MySQL binaries could be damaged, deleted, or altered.
E. Extra startup time would be required for the MySQL server to reset the privileges.

Correct Answer: B, E

40. User account baduser@hostname on your MySQL instance has been compromised.
Which two commands stop any new connections using the compromised account? (Choose two.)
A. ALTER USER baduser@hostname PASSWORD DISABLED;
B. ALTER USER baduser@hostname MAX_USER_CONNECTIONS 0;
C. ALTER USER baduser@hostname ACCOUNT LOCK;
D. ALTER USER baduser@hostname IDENTIFIED WITH mysql_no_login;
E. ALTER USER baduser@hostname DEFAULT ROLE NONE;
Correct Answer: C, D

41. An existing asynchronous replication setup is running MySQL 8.
Which two steps are a part of implementing GTID replication? (Choose two.)
A. Enable GTID by executing this on the master and the slave: SET GLOBAL GTID_ENABLED=on;
B. Execute this on the slave to enable GTID: START SLAVE IO_THREAD WITH GTID;
C. Restart MySQL (master and slave) with these options enabled:
--gtid_mode=ON
--log-bin
--log-slave-updates
--enforce-gtid-consistency
D. Execute this on the slave to enable GTID: RESET SLAVE; START SLAVE GTID_NEXT=AUTOMATIC;
E. On the slave, alter the MySQL master connection setting with: ALTER channel CHANGE MASTER TO MASTER_AUTO_POSITION = 1;
F. On the slave, alter the MySQL master connection setting with: CHANGE MASTER TO MASTER_AUTO_POSITION = 1;

Correct Answer: C, F

42. Which four connection methods can MySQL clients specify with the --protocol option when connecting to a MySQL server? (Choose four.)
A. TCP
B. SOCKET
C. PIPE
D. DIRECT
E. IPv6
F. FILE
G. IPv4
H. MEMORY

Correct Answer: A, B, C, H

43. Examine this command and output:

Which two statements are true? (Choose two.)
A. The lock is at the metadata object level.
B. The lock is a shared lock.
C. The lock is an intentional lock.
D. The lock is at the table object level.
E. The lock is a row-level lock.
F. The lock is an exclusive lock.

Correct Answer: D, F

44. Which two statements are true about general tablespaces?
(Choose two)
A. General tablespaces support temporary tables.

B. Dropping a table from a general tablespace releases the space back to the operating system.
C. An existing table can be moved into a general tablespace
D. A general tablespace can have multiple data files.
E. A new table can be created explicitly in a general tablespace.

Correct Answer: C, E

45. Which three statements are true about MySQL replication? (Choose three.)
A. Replication can use only TCP/IP connections.
B. Any instance can have multiple slaves, but it can have only one master.
C. Each instance in a replication topology must have a unique server ID.
D. Binary logs contain only transactions originating from a single MySQL instance.
E. Each slave must have its own MySQL user for replication.
F. Binary logging must be enabled on the master in order to replicate to other instances.
G. A replication user must have the SELECT privilege for all tables that need to be replicated.

Correct Answer: C, F, G

46. Which two statements are true about the mysql_config_editor program? (Choose two.)
A. It manages the configuration of the MySQL Firewall feature.
B. It manages the configuration of client programs.
C. It can move datadir to a new location.
D. It manages the configuration of user privileges for accessing the server.
E. It will use [client] options by default unless you provide --login-path.
F. It can be used to create and edit SSL certificates and log locations.
G. It provides an interface to change my.cnf files.

Correct Answer: B, E

47. What does the binlog dump thread do?
A. It monitors and schedules the rotation/deletion of the binary logs.
B. It acquires a lock on the binary log for reading each event to be sent to the slave.
C. It connects to the master and asks it to send updates recorded in its binary logs.
D. It reads the relay log and executes the events contained in them.
Correct Answer: C

48. Examine this command, which executes successfully:
shell> mysqldump --master-data=2 --single-transaction --result-file=dump.sql mydb
Which two statements are true? (Choose two.)
A. It executes flush tables with read lock.
B. It enforces consistent backups for all storage engines.
C. The backup created is a consistent data dump.
D. This option uses the READ COMMITTED transaction isolation mode.
E. It is a cold backup.

Correct Answer: A, D

49. Examine this query and output:

Which two statements are true? (Choose two.)
A. The country table is accessed as the first table, and then joined to the city table.
B. It takes more than 8 milliseconds to sort the rows.
C. The optimizer estimates that 51 rows in the country table have Continent = 'Asia'.
D. 35 rows from the city table are included in the result.
E. The query returns exactly 125 rows.

Correct Answer: C, D

50. Examine this command, which executes successfully:
mysqlpump -–user=root --password > full_backup.sql
Which two databases will be excluded from this dump? (Choose two.)
A. information_schema
B. world
C. employee

D. sys
E. mysql

Correct Answer: A, D

51. Identify two ways to significantly improve data security.
(Choose two)
A. Configure mysqld to run as the system admin account, such as root.
B. Use a private network behind a firewall.
C. Configure mysqld to use only networked disks.
D. Configure MySQL to have only one administrative account.
E. Configure mysqld to use only local disks or attached disks and to have its own account in the host system.
Correct Answer: B, E

52. Examine this MySQL client command to connect to a remote database: mysql -h remote.example.org -u root -p --protocol=TCP --ssl-mode=
Which two --ssl-mode values will ensure that an X.509-compliant certificate will be used to establish the SSL/TLS connection to MySQL?
A. REQUIRED
B. VERIFY_CA
C. VERIFY_IDENTITY
D. PREFERRED
E. DISABLED

Correct Answer: A

53. our want to log only the changes made to the database objects and data on the MySQL system.
Which log will do this by default?
A. general query log
B. audit log
C. slow query log
D. binary log
E. error log

Correct Answer: D

54. Which two statements are true about using backups of the binary log? (Choose two.)
A. Multiple binary logs can be used to restore data.
B. Multiple binary logs can be applied in parallel for faster data restoration.
C. Binary logs are relatively small, and therefore, excellent for long-term storage and disaster recovery.
D. Binary logs can always be used to unapply unwanted schema changes.
E. They allow for point-in-time recovery of the data.

Correct Answer: D, E

55. Where is the default data directory located after installing MySQL using RPM on Oracle Linux 7?
A. /usr/mysql
B. /usr/bin
C. /etc/my.cnf
D. /var/lib/mysql
E. /usr

Correct Answer: B

56. A user wants to connect without entering his or her username and password on the Linux command prompt.
Which three locations can be used to store the user's mysql credentials to satisfy this requirement? (Choose three.)
A. $HOME/.my.cnf file
B. $MYSQL_HOME/my.cnf file
C. DATADIR/mysqld-auto.cnf file
D. $HOME/.mylogin.cnf file
E. $HOME/.mysql/auth/login file
F. /etc/my.cnf file
G. $HOME/.mysqlrc file

Correct Answer: B, C, F

57. It is a non-empty InnoDB table.
Examine these statements, which are executed in one session:
BEGIN;
SELECT * FROM t FOR UPDATE;
Which is true?
A. If OPTIMIZE TABLE; is invoked, it will create a table lock on t and force a transaction rollback.
B. If OPTIMIZE LOCAL TABLE t; is invoked from another session, it executes normally and returns the status.
C. mysqlcheck --analyze --all-databases will execute normally on all tables and return a report.
D. If ANALYZE TABLE; is invoked from the same session, it hangs until the transaction is committed or rolled back.
Correct Answer: B

58. Where is the default data directory located after installing MySQL using RPM on Oracle Linux 7?
(Choose one)
A. /usr
B. /usr/mysql
C. /etc/my.cnf
D. /var/1ib/mysql
E. /usr/bin
Correct Answer: D

59. Which two MySQL Server accounts are locked by default? (Choose two.)
A. any user set as DEFINER for stored programs
B. any internal system accounts
C. any new ROLE accounts
D. any user created without a password
E. any user created with a username, but missing the host name

Correct Answer: A, B

60. Examine this SQL statement:

Which set of privileges will allow Tom to execute this SQL statement?
A. GRANT ALL PRIVILEGES ON 'world'.'city' TO 'tom'@'%';
GRANT SELECT ('code') ON 'world'.'country' TO 'tom'@'%';
B. GRANT UPDATE ON 'world'.* TO 'tom'@'%';
GRANT ALL PRIVILEGES ON 'world'.'country' TO 'tom'@'%';
C. GRANT UPDATE ON 'world'.'city' TO 'tom'@'%';
GRANT SELECT ON 'world'.* TO 'tom'@'%';
D. GRANT UPDATE ON 'world'.'city' TO 'tom'@'%';
GRANT SELECT ON 'world'.'country' TO 'tom'@'%';

Correct Answer: D

61. Examine these commands and output:

Which connection ID is holding the metadata lock?
A. 20
B. 24
C. 21
D. 25
E. 22
F. 6

Correct Answer: D

62. Examine the command, which executes successfully: shell> mysqld --initialize
Which statement is true?
(Choose one)
A. The root password is created in the error log in plain text.
B. The installation creates a temporary test environment with data in the /tmp directory.
C. The installation is created without enforcing or generating SSL certificates.
D. The root password is not created allowing easy access from the same host.

Correct Answer: A

63. Which two are true about binary logs used in asynchronous replication? (Choose two.)
A. They are pushed from the master to the slave.
B. They contain events that describe database changes on the master.
C. They contain events that describe all queries run on the master.
D. They contain events that describe only administrative commands run on the master.
E. They are pulled from the master to the slave.

Correct Answer: A, B

64. Which two queries are examples of successful SQL injection attacks? (Choose two.)
A. SELECT user,passwd FROM members -
WHERE user = '?';INSERT INTO members('user','passwd') VALUES ('bob@example.com','secret');--';
B. SELECT id, name FROM user WHERE user.id=(SELECT members.id FROM members);
C. SELECT id, name FROM user WHERE id=23 OR id=32 OR 1=1;
D. SELECT id, name FROM user WHERE id=23 OR id=32 AND 1=1;
E. SELECT email,passwd FROM members
WHERE email = 'INSERT INTO members('email','passwd') VALUES ('bob@example.com', 'secret');--';
F. SELECT user, phone FROM customers WHERE name = '\; DROP TABLE users; --';

Correct Answer: D, E

65. You execute this command:
shell> mysqlpump --exclude-databases=% --users
Which statement is true?
A. It creates a logical backup of all MySQL user accounts.
B. It creates a logical backup of all metadata, but contains no table data.
C. It returns an error because the mysqldump command should have been used.
D. It creates a logical backup of only the users database.

Correct Answer: B

66. Which two are contained in the InnoDB system tablespace (ibdata1) by default? (Chose two.)
A. table data
B. primary indexes
C. user privileges
D. InnoDB Data Dictionary
E. change buffer
F. doublewrite buffer

Correct Answer: D, F

67. Which two MySQL Shell commands are excluded from the InnoDB Cluster creation procedure? (Choose two.)
A. dba.configureInstance()
B. cluster.setPrimaryInstance()
C. dba.configureLocalInstance()
D. cluster.forceQuorumUsingPartitionOf()
E. cluster.addInstance()
F. dba.createCluster()
G. dba.checkInstanceConfiguration()

Correct Answer: B, D

68. On examination, your MySQL installation datadir has become recursively world read/write/executable. What are two major concerns of running an installation with incorrect file privileges?
(Choose two.)
A. Data files could be deleted.
B. Extra startup time would be required for the MySQL server to reset the privileges.
C. MySQL binaries could be damaged, deleted, or altered.
D. SQL injections could be used to insert bad data into the database.
E. Users could overwrite configuration files.

Correct Answer: A, B

69. Examine this statement:
mysql> DROP ROLE r_role1, r_role2;
Which two are true? (Choose two.)
A. It fails if any of the roles is specified in the mandatory_roles variable.
B. You must revoke r_role1 and r_role2 from all users and other roles before dropping the roles.
C. Existing connections can continue to use the roles' privileges until they reconnect.
D. You must revoke all privileges from r_role1 and r_role2 before dropping the roles.
E. It fails if you do not have the ADMIN OPTION of the roles r_role1 and r_role2.
F. It fails if at least one of the roles does not exist.

Correct Answer: C, E

70. Examine these statements and output:

Which statement is true?
A. The user is logged in with --user=accounting as an option.
B. The user is authenticated as the anonymous proxy user ''@'%'.
C. The user is authorized as the accounting@localhost user.
D. The user is authorized as the rsmith@localhost user.
E. The user failed to define a username and the connecting username defaulted to ''@'%'.

Correct Answer: D

71. How can mysql_multi be configured to allow MySQL instances to use the same port number? (Choose one)
A. The instances listen on different IP addresses
B. The instances use different user accounts unique teach instance.
C. The instances use different socket names
D. The instances have appropriate net masks set.

Correct Answer: A

72. Which two statements are true about InnoDB data-at-rest encryption? (Choose two.)
A. It supports only non-blob datatypes.
B. It does not support the transportable tablespaces feature.
C. It supports all indexes transparently.
D. It decrypts data for use in memory.
E. It enforces encryption from disk to memory and over network transmission.

Correct Answer: C, D

73. You plan to install MySQL Server by using the RPM download.
Which two statements are true? (Choose two.)
A. You can provide the root password interactively.
B. You must manually initialize the data directory.
C. The MySQL RPM package installation supports deploying multiple MySQL versions on the same host.
D. MySQL uses the RPM relocatable installation target feature.
E. The functionality is split among several RPM package files.
F. You can find the root password in the error log after the first start.

Correct Answer: C, F

ONLINE RESOURCES

Practice Paper
Link: https://forms.gle/VG5pMtNVoMDFL5z46
QR Code:

Video Content:

Link: https://www.youtube.com/playlist?list=PLzlh_31VWEFqnSgKTZk4bfnZ2Cjaapzi4
QR Code:

ADDITIONAL RESOURCE

MySQL Textbook Playlist
Link: https://www.youtube.com/playlist?list=PLzlh_31VWEFoTeJV8A69kyiPllGDoeD7Y
QR Code:

YouTube Videos Playlists for all Chapters

Chapter 1:
Link: https://www.youtube.com/playlist?list=PLzlh_31VWEFob91YvVOqYVtTg2-OgJMQ5
QR Code:

Chapter 2:
Link: https://www.youtube.com/playlist?list=PLzlh_31VWEFrxCQZ9ZXZ7AllrLd7KhCks
QR Code:

Chapter 3:
Link: https://www.youtube.com/playlist?list=PLzlh_31VWEFrZIhNdZoLo6IUk6iy0PGEv
QR Code:

Chapter 4:
Link: https://www.youtube.com/playlist?list=PLzlh_31VWEFp6Rk5MmSOYtphClAq7D05J
QR Code:

Chapter 5:
Link: https://www.youtube.com/playlist?list=PLzlh_31VWEFp7iVY0eeEGf-Kj6hG2U2wh
QR Code:

Chapter 6:
Link: https://www.youtube.com/playlist?list=PLzlh_31VWEFoNLO-nMGMAO166a_WRC4-0
QR Code:

Chapter 7:
Link: https://www.youtube.com/playlist?list=PLzlh_31VWEFp5Ra5jTT_FKmdDPILuwN05
QR Code:

Chapter 8:
Link: https://www.youtube.com/playlist?list=PLzlh_31VWEFpAYiYYNVrSqr7hsrIcxSSO
QR Code:

Chapter 9:
Link: https://www.youtube.com/playlist?list=PLzlh_31VWEFqEaja4Jqbe3YFLxNAPMMe4
QR Code:

Chapter 10:
Link: https://www.youtube.com/playlist?list=PLzlh_31VWEFqBCnbj1-XKKcftPVRZ8UAO
QR Code:

Chapter 11:
Link: https://www.youtube.com/playlist?list=PLzlh_31VWEFrNXWdsOnKsF5bIRE8CTJmA
QR Code:

Chapter 12:
Link: https://www.youtube.com/playlist?list=PLzlh_31VWEFpXHvD6vus_FDFpsRLkzjxf
QR Code:

Chapter 13:
Link: https://www.youtube.com/playlist?list=PLzlh_31VWEFrxU0fHSnKF1abVw4I0PLRQ
QR Code:

Chapter 14:
Link: https://www.youtube.com/playlist?list=PLzlh_31VWEFqnSgKTZk4bfnZ2Cjaapzi4
QR Code:

Microsoft SQL Server Interview Questions & Answers Playlist.
Link: https://www.youtube.com/playlist?list=PLzlh_31VWEFrmxI7adv506EZqlvAbVnrL
QR Code:

Microsoft SQL Server Playlist.
Link: https://www.youtube.com/playlist?list=PLzlh_31VWEFow9PqL3ITYtqvt3JkYojZw
QR Code:

MySQL Interview book Playlist.
Link: https://www.youtube.com/playlist?list=PLzlh_31VWEFoXDE1sZYwytXr0w7oxsghn
QR Code: